Tequila Sunrise
for Business

The combination of three key ingredients to take your
business to the level you want to achieve

Acnowledgments

To each and every one of the people who with their intention, no matter what it was, helped to get this project.

Dedications

To my beloved daughters: Alanna & Astrid Flores, the most valuable beings in my life. Their mere existence illuminates my path.

Content

Tequila Sunrise
for Business

Introduction
The intention of this cocktail

The only way to do a great work is to love what you do
STEVE JOBS
American entrepreneur, marketer and inventor

The metaphorical combination of this book represents only, in a simple form, the basis on which the power of life is expressed to create reality in business. In its ancestral ingredients that exist in all the parts and it is possible to recognize, it is encrypted the formula that by analogy I have called Tequila Sunrise for its easy assimilation.

By its nature, the strength of these ingredients has been incorporated in the largest companies throughout history proving to keep the commercial system that we have developed successfully active. And I have concentrated them here so that you learn to delight them by making them part of the foundations of your business.

The Tequila Sunrise aims to make you the infusion of foundations, develop its processes and recognize the vehicles that are characteristic of these three ingredients. That may you adopt the positive way of creating a reality of abundance by recognizing the characteristics, qualities and doses of this metaphorical energy concoction. And that their energy can serve you so much to emerge, excel, and be certain to last in business by keeping the operation of any business in action.

The ingredients that represents to the Tequila Sunrise on business have evolved with a particular purpose: get everything that every big successful company has wanted. And they have had a common sense: that well combined they have proved to be the great force that makes companies work effectively to make succeed in business.

Well, they represent the fundamentals that, one: by themselves complete the energy that moves any project. Two: they move businesses in general in the current commercial system. And here I tell you clearly, three: you will know in order that you acting in consequence of your ideas in particular can carry out the project you wish to achieve.

In the process of serving the three ingredients that shape the Tequila Sunrise for Business, it must take into account the importance and function that takes the ice cubes as the basis of the cocktail ingredients, that every enterprise must know pouring into your business as a catalyst, to understand how its freezing temperature develops best qualities to the objective you want to see reflected in material reality; thus, giving temper to the mix.

This cold ingredient emphasizes its action: Since the beginning of the elaboration: to be planted with the solid presence that will act in the ingredients. During preparation: to maintain the important temperature required for the cocktail. And until the end of the tasting: to obtain the expected results it produces its effect.

That is, throughout the realization of any business project, by the fact that it achieves the desired effect only by impregnating its cold temperature in the three ingredients of the cocktail, and when these are poured into it, in the correct order as here is posed.

And it is along the preparation of the cocktail, that the ice cubes are developing its characteristic qualities in its most pure expression.

Qualities that must be present and must act to correctly precise all business movements; they indicate how to let at their best the delicate preparation of the Tequila Sunrise for Business. And you will be glimpsing on in each ingredient.

Likewise, you will learn from some points of view of various authors, specific studies on these main ingredients used in business, and the most outstanding rules that have followed some of the most important businessmen with whom they have achieved success in their business activity, and you will do it based on diagrams that will help you learn these ingredients.

For finally, you realize that the correct preparation of this combined elixir in your business causes a unique effect, that from the mind of your company rises to that of your consumer like the Sunrise Effect.

And once there, allow yourself to understand how to drive the direction of business that you want, so that from now on, those around you and the consumer learn to distinguish the moments when this effect is going up in their mind, in such a way, that causes them win in their life and to you in business.

It depends heavily on the correct combination of the Tequila Sunrise for Business, so that your firm is well endowed with all its qualities and that one to one conformed in your projects and thus you can achieve with them the effect they need, since only with the will to go for what you want you can get the preparation, revelation, and the result you require in your business.

That is, that upon reaching the complete visualization of how to configure your company with the Tequila Sunrise for Business; one, you will understand how to develop your projects; two, you will control how to position a product properly; and three, you will notice the effect that can have when it rises in the mind and influences in the decision of purchase of the consumer, by acting promptly in the decisive moments in which your projects and your business they are followed by many people. For now, in general, you correctly achieve your major business objectives. Seeing thus their material results as a consequence of success and getting what you want to achieve.

The objective of the Tequila Sunrise for Business is that you fully develop its ingredients entwined by the necessary ice, as it has three important purposes: one: to achieve full abundance through the way you make a living, that is, to achieve the well-being of the organization of your business; two: that you strengthen genuine exchange through the forms of commercialization of the context, that is, that you achieve the well-being of the market in your sector; and three: that you get better results in the development of your product, or that you achieve true well-being in the life of the consumer; because together they are related within the commercial system in which we live to a global trend and need in the most conscious, profound and authentic way: to dominate in business with the Tequila Sunrise for Business.

Knowing the legend

A good product can last forever
BERNARD ARNAULT
French billionaire business magnate, and art collector

_____

One of the secrets it holds life within each of the entities it creates, is clearly marked in a cocktail that is well known by all; of course, I mean the Tequila Sunrise. This drink keeps visibly defined its special combination, and into the quality of each of its ingredients, by the combined effect, they are accurately reflected the functions it has to play any company to achieve success.

Life always evolves to create, achieve success and leave history.

The presence of tequila goes from tradition to the law by the time of the Mexican Revolution when Porfirio Diaz organized to promote the drink called "mezcal wine" at a fair in San Antonio Texas to that in that place they called wine tequila for the location which came.

There are references since 1943 to protect the name "tequila" and to obtain the exclusivity of use, focusing on a long history associated with the region's industry, the town and the hill with this drink. Since 1958, Mexico protected designations of origin and their international registration.

Designation of Origin (DO) is the name of a geographical region that serves to designate a product originating therein and whose quality or characteristics are due exclusively to the geographical environment. Products with designation of origin in the world cannot be produced in any more side than its original place. Worldwide, only 187 municipalities in five states in Mexico are allowed and can produce tequila. Designation of Origin Tequila (DOT) comprises all municipalities Jalisco and some of Michoacan, Nayarit, Guanajuato and Tamaulipas. This means that all drinks called tequila, both in Mexico and abroad, should come from factories in this region, under the supervision of the *Consejo Regulador del Tequila (CRT)* [Tequila Regulatory Council]. So, no one can use the Designation of Origin Tequila, which is the word tequila, to distinguish any product, if not authorized by the Mexican government, through the institution designated to protect it, which in this case is the CRT.

Mexico has the Designation of Origin Tequila, and it is considered the national drink.

The tequila industry is seeking exclusive use of the word agave for tequila in their bottles. This means excluding others that sell industrial products with the same raw material. Therefore, argue that exist in the market beverages even when made from the agave plant are not only distilled entirely made with blue variety *wever* kind *tequilana*. The consumer buys drinks thinking it's a real blue agave tequila, without being so.

Note that to this effort also meet producers of other non-generic or distilled beverages, which are also made with agave. In the case of *mezcal* and *bacanora*, they also are affected by brands that use reputation built for these products.

Therefore, we must know the different kinds of tequila that are five and a go from low to high maturity: white, young, rested, aged and extra aged. And to be considered 100 percent agave must be of a single species of this plant without mixing with other species of agave.

The tequila houses and its more than 200 years of tradition reinforce its presence to see consolidated its recognition in the international market.

Already for the sixties tequila it is relatively famous in the world and especially in some countries like Japan and Spain. Since 1973 the General Declaration of Protection of the Designation of Origin "Tequila" is requested. An agreement between Mexico and the US establishes by which Mexico agrees in preventing the use of the name "Bourbon" within its territory and the US public the recognition to Tequila as a distinctive and exclusive product of Mexico in the Federal Register. In 1974 Canada restricts the use of Tequila name to products from Mexico, and the Mexican government granted the protection to the Designation of Origin Tequila. In 1977 the territory of Designation of Origin is extended to some municipalities of Tamaulipas.

In 1978 the certificate of registration of Tequila is obtained in the "Registre International des Appelations D'origine" of the World Intellectual Property Organization (Geneva, Switzerland). In 1981 the

Province of Quebec (Canada) expressed appreciation to the DOT. Denmark in 1982 recognizes the DOT but it has taken years recognition from other countries. In Russia is obtained in 2012.

Today, tequila has one of the highest standards of quality and prestige. And it certainly ranks as one of the most recognized beverages produced in Mexico and sold around the world. The history of tequila and their houses are closely related, as their tequila dynasties are so old that today, this famous liqueur, is one of the most grounded in the Mexican and international markets.

The market for tequila in Mexico is on the Tequila region par excellence which is 'el Bajio', however the heartland concentrates largely in consumption by population density. Approximately 60 percent of consumers in Mexico prefer to take it as tequila cocktail Paloma. Approximately 100 000 Palomas are consumed per hour.

America is the country's best-selling tequila over Mexico with an approximate consumption of 11 million boxes. Higher consumption is generated in USA through the cocktail Margarita, with approximately 200 000 Margaritas per hour consumed.

Tequila is one of the best cards of Mexico in the world and its unique flavor is increasingly sought in international markets. (*Revistafortuna*; *Consejo Regulador del Tequila*, 2013)

According to Manjunath Reddy, a lead alcoholic beverages research expert from Technavio a leading global research and advisory firm with global coverage and headquarters in London, UK, in its global market research report on tequila for 2017-2021. "Consumers are demanding innovative and exotic flavors in their drinks. The introduction of new flavors by major players to cater to the changing taste preference of consumers is boosting the demand for tequila […] An increase in endorsements by celebrities, development of innovative packaging techniques, and growing online retail is expected to propel the growth of the market." (Business Wire, 2017)

Tequila Sunrise was coined by Gene Sulit, a former employee who worked at the Arizona Biltmore Hotel by various occupations between the decades 1930 and 1940, during his time as a bartender, after one of his regular customers asked for a cocktail, combining his love for the Tequila with his preference for taste drinks poolside. The story can be found in detail in the resort's Wright bar. (Phoenixnewtimes, 2015)

Tequila Sunrise which was created and served for the first time originally contained (tequila, crème de cassis, lemon juice and soda water).

The modern Tequila Sunrise is a cocktail made of tequila, orange juice, and grenadine syrup and served unmixed in a tall glass with ice cubes.

This drink was originated from California in the early 1970s and was created by Bobby Lazoff and Billy Rice while working as young bartenders at the Trident in Sausalito, California north of San Francisco.

The cocktail is named for its appearance when served, with gradations of color resembling a sunrise.

And here is contained the relation that this one cocktail has with business, it is in evolution; once obtained, it is very important to achieve the characteristic flavor and effect of Tequila Sunrise, by activating the combined power that their ingredients have. Evolution that in a company, is the result of achieving the differentiation, the leadership and financial independence, present to properly activate their ingredients through the role of its organs, which have aim to develop the combination of their qualities secret to obtain the Sunrise on your business.

In 1972, at a private party at the Trident organized by Bill Graham to kick off the Rolling Stones' 1972 tour in America, Mick Jagger had one of the cocktails, liked it, and he and his entourage started drinking them down. They later ordered them all across America, even dubbing the tour itself their "cocaine and tequila sunrise tour." (Wikipedia.org, 2015).

In my opinion, that decision changed the reality and manifests something unique. From this success is treated, to have the decision to achieve a goal with the intention of creating a new reality, which, with determination has such a different mark, that it becomes special.

Of the Tequila Sunrise for Business

My biggest motivation? Just to keep challenging myself
RICHARD BRANSON
English businessman and investor

This creation begins by feeling the force of nature projected in business.

Mexico City. 1999. Two years after university. Design Business Professor. The sun rises, the party abounds, marketing surrounds you, business captivates and yet ... life creates ... Observing the possibilities: To raise the sun and reflect life.

I still rejoiced visiting the *Academia de San Carlos* [San Carlos Academy] and the then *Escuela Nacional de Artes Plásticas* [National School of Plastic Arts]. I like to finish what I start. Taste for being self-taught in business and design. Human potential thought motivator. Especially passionate about ecological sustainable technology businesses, health care businesses with a naturist methodology, as well as, fashion businesses with an emphasis on the natural forefront.

Since I didn't have a job, one day I closed my eyes and I only saw myself doing what was easiest for me and immediately I slept. Three days later, I went out with the intention of finding the best. My journey started from behind the *Anahuacalli* Museum, walking, by train, and subway to the Roma neighborhood. And on my way, I found Carl an old friend that I hadn't seen for years. He had just left his job a few hours ago, I told him about my search and he took me to relieve him.

My life had changed to become exciting.

From there we walked to the *Zona Rosa* area. *Insurgentes* roundabout. *Nice Street*. An eclectic construction between Art Nouveau and Belle Époque, with one wooden door after another glass door that were open was the work residence.

Opening the air through the face and going up.

A curved wooden staircase led us to an anteroom with a large chandelier. A man of great charisma in all aspects 'Pavarotti' style received us.

By saying 'Pavarotti' style I mean with respect to his great physical resemblance and dressing with the famous Italian lyrical tenor.

There, my contact introduced us and the three of us quickly talked about my interest in my insertion into the institution.

–Carl, since when do you know your possible successor? –asked 'Pavarotti'.

–He is from *ENAP* [National School of Plastic Arts] –said Carl quietly.

And as if by magic he told me the previous conditions to be met:

–Have you taught before? –He asked.

–Yes. Individuals, small groups of students, illustration and computing. –I replied.

–Are you hired elsewhere?

–No.

–You have free all the week?

–Yes.

–Would you be willing to register with the Treasury for fees?

–Yes.

He asks me to give a sample class for arrivals at 1:00 p.m. I accepted quickly. We said goodbye.

My friend Carl left in a hurry and I went to get my class ready in a coffee. The one with three owls. I had no money to buy a marker or large sheet of paper, any more than to pay for a coffee and my return ticket. I sat at an empty table with a forgotten newspaper. I ordered the classic cheap coffee. That newspaper helped me to find headings for articles about the city, fashion and business, which I imaginatively related to a specific topic until I put together a full one-hour class. I went through everything mentally. I didn't know what the class topic was going to be. So, the three articles served as my start, development, and conclusions, tailored to what class it might be.

An hour and a half passed. The time was coming. I paid and went to the institution. Just one block on the way. Music going out of business. Foreigners in restaurants. Traffic on wheels. People walking everywhere. Approaching. The red-yellow store. The music store. Wood and glass doors. Climbing the stairs with a beating heart and newspaper in hand. Taking a deep breath. Handshake. Flicker.

–Come over here –'Pavarotti' said to me.

-Yes, thank you -I replied and followed after a glass separation. Approximately 5 meters.

-Very good. This room is waiting for us. You have a blackboard and three-color markers. Give me an Advertising class -he said.

He sat down and I started introducing myself quickly as a teacher. Immediately the kind of topic that first came to my mind. BTL and its role in the city. I wore it for about 10 minutes when I heard his voice.

-Now tell me about Photography.

-Yes, of course … I resumed my position. I sighed deeply. Half of the board. I marked a vertical line. "This subject is about photo frames" -I said.

After about 5 minutes he raised his voice with the phrase: "ready."

-Yes? -I asked for.

-It's enough. This is the food space and I want to take advantage of it. Do you have something else to say? -he concluded.

-No… Thank you for having attended to me. -I said ready to leave and fluctuating my mind between "I think everything is over" and "now what will I do" I began to erase the board.

It was about 15 endless seconds while at the same time he got up, opened the door, stood firm looking at me, I followed him out, he turned off the light and closed the room. We made our way to his large desk bar. I stood up front. He sat down and checked his PC.

"You're hired" -he said confidently and quickly.

-It's okay. When can I start? -I answered surprised and excited.

-Since today. Your first class starts at 5:00 p.m. Each class is one and a half hours. Your schedule to meet is four days a week, some hours in the morning and others in the afternoon. This is your schedule and your classes. Come prepared with your food. I require your commitment and your punctuality. Here I will tell you what is missing -he said.

We said goodbye. I waited a few hours in the same owl store in their magazine section, hunger faded, there I reviewed the classes that first day to plan them in the same imaginary way. I supported myself by taking inspiration from the most related magazines and books that I could. The time came and I immediately showed up to start teaching.

An exciting uncertainty that made me feel like winning a lot tackled me from that first day. They were all different. I passed the end of the quarter. And it came from one day to the next, the next quarter of year.

Lounges really full. 40 average students per class. Full schedule. High passion. Polishing skills. Release to the max. Fantastic profit.

January 2000. I got married. Now it is little profit. Looking for better opportunities I changed jobs.

Two old acquaintances; an 'trickster' who 9 years ago he asked me to give him an illustration of me as a personal gift, which then seemed flattering to me, although he did not give me anything in return, and some 3 years ago, a 'family business owner' Who sought me out by commissioning me a design with features of the Mexican Caribbean without talking about pay, which I did not do because of my university studies; the second person, looked for me again due to my recent marriage offering me a job in their 'family business'. Their business model? Making and graphic design of tourist shirts for the Riviera Maya. The first-person, sending greetings.

The deal was, you work for us, a meager salary, without legal benefits and without a contract, but with an unfurnished home nearby, for a year and you live surrounded by peace in a paradisiacal place, and in time, you will be released alone. That was told to me by the 'family business owner' himself.

Of course I asked myself, why does the person who offers me the job condition me from the beginning by saying to me: "work for me doing as many drawings as possible and I pay you 'x low price' a week, but without hiring you"; limiting my personal and professional development?

That is not honest. But it is clear why people are not honest: Because they confuse doing business with cheating, they do not know how to base themselves on what is valuable or successful, nor do they know that everything works with the win-win relationship. They cannot understand it and do not know how to do it. Whoever directs himself has to improve his behavior or everything machined is returned to them.

With the certainty of my professional ethics, my creativity and learning from this experience to achieve my success, I agreed. Welcome Yucatan.

But at work, the 'trickster,' the person who had mainly asked me for that illustration; every opportunity he had he tried to rush me, ask me his doubts and then correct me. He constantly ended up saying to himself out loud: "I just don't have a personality." He kept looking for attention telling the 'family business owner' and the 'family business manager' that they did not do their job well, and he had better ideas, to which he received the unanimous response from them: "Whoever says that shows it". Very unusual traits that do not precisely determine a healthy business environment. Nor in personal development, with that powerful solvent smell spread all over the place, something that goes against the environment and health.

Leaving that aside, I was fascinated by several things about the workplace, although modest, being able to carry out my design process on a computer for my personal use, feel the atmosphere of collaborating designing in doing business for the Riviera Maya and the air conditioning that offered the office. From the outside, living more independently surrounded by a very different culture.

By then I was already listening in the office of a strong 'free seller', who, for some reason, without both knowing us, he tried to greet me every time he visited the place. But, the approach to my person was also from another side, with a 'free marketer' close to the business and merchant of garments who added the design.

The insistence was sporadic and increasing for a couple of months.

One day the 'free marketer' acted quickly and offered me to design for he. I told him that we would probably see him later, we did not close any deals.

One day they celebrated a meeting with great food and music, to which the hired workers of the place, friends of the business, and a server like 'freelancer' attended; where there was also the much-mentioned 'free seller' who, when I went to the bar to help myself to drink, he was encouraged to approach to immediately try to give me a short flattering talk about my design style. Someone spokes to him, he continued that talk, and that interrupted us.

Either way, I was not going to serve or could more than one business. Who offered me a job first, was my priority. Also, it seemed to me that there was dishonest competition in the place, in order to hoard whoever was helping them to succeed in their businesses without due respect to any of the parties known among them.

It was hard enough dealing with the heat and humidity so strong and suddenly lasting for me, the fulfillment of my work and my commitment at home as a newlywed, to focus on meeting other people's business goals. And the 'free marketer' was already starting to visit me to convince me at home. I saw myself accomplished in my own business, in something different from all that.

Suddenly, everything accelerated at the end of May of that year.

Well, after several visits to private medical offices for a constant discomfort in who was my then partner, and seeing her decline more and more in her mood and physical state, according to the doctor for hormonal changes and resenting the abrupt change of climate at being outsiders, as a couple, we received the beautiful news that we were expecting our first daughter.

I did not have an employment contract or legal benefits, my then partner dehydrating and losing weight continued to feel increasingly ill, and when her health was really worse, one day I simply left everything and returned with her to Mexico City. Of course, I apologized to the 'family business owner'.

Although a few weeks passed, fortunately, in my previous job I was given the opportunity for the second time to become passionate again. So, I was giving classes on the performance of design in business. Getting involved, researching, finding the points that make businesses work integrally. And at the same time, giving me the task of supporting the best possible care of the pregnancy of the mother of my children and, also, in the postpartum period of my first daughter.

By 2002, I was still a teacher and already started publishing ads in specialized magazines offering my professional design services. At the end of that year, I found out about the support that the then CDMX government was providing to the MSMEs in the city. I did everything to profile myself, I attended the entrepreneur training courses so that each enrollee could develop a business plan.

I expanded as I like, getting to the bottom of things to do what I can to achieve what you want. Between part-time classes, the development of the business plan, and the coexistence with the family hardly gave me time to sleep.

This is how I progressed in the business plan, from the market study to the corporate ID manual. To later detail the editorial calendar, the magazine design and RP logistics. I was working thoroughly on my project until it was taking shape. I invested months of development and a great pleasure in doing it.

In 2003, I managed to be accepted into another institution and I continued fighting for what we all seek to improve. I was still working part-time and contacting potential advertisers to whom I was proposing my project, a medium that would converge the products of large emporiums with consumer preferences.

Everything was slow, but it seemed to be going well.

When I already had the foundations to get the right work team and support the mother of my children during their bachelor's degree, things in family began to fail. This happens when there is no compatibility in the ways of working hard to achieve prosperity.

If you are with a person who does not respect or respond to the commitment to excellence, with that person it is not possible to achieve success, which requires actively keeping your life project in view with the professional purpose of achieving objectives. Your commitment to excellence extends to social circles from all aspects of your life, in each person who is related to the project you undertake.

It is a very important requirement to develop professionally, share your goals, keep them in view, meet them together and achieve your goals.

In 2004, the family of three left, with the great joy of knowing that a male member of the family was on the way, on a trip to Yucatan to visit my parents. They were neighbors of the 'family business' of shirts that I had previously tried. It would work for me to try to clear my mind. And now, as short as that spreading was, I wanted to enjoy it and clear myself of the great burden of stress.

Of course, I met again with people who once wanted me to work for them, and they immediately tried to commission new designs from me in order to help them make these, the closest thing to a very realistic, innovative technique they had encountered by the website of an

American company. I was not on a work plan. And professionalism, good work and innovation have just their time and value, which not many are willing to understand or pay for. Good and deep things don't work with "something quick."

And, in addition, the 'family business owner' escalated the tone saying: "You know, without a contract, you make many good drawings, and I only pay you for the drawing that they tell me works for them."

The short time that my family and I would be there would not be enough to rest from work and work at the same time. Unfortunately, we live in a society in which the vast majority of people do not know how to hear or understand a "I cannot, thank you" even if you explain the reasons, because they take it negatively and offensively anyway.

Of course, it was a great challenge. I analyzed the proposal for days. And although I am a design professional, my intention has never been to dedicate myself to the same thing that they do, so we do not close any deal about it. My direction raises other limits very mine with very great purposes for me.

Returning home to Mexico City I continued to pursue success. I supported the mother of my children in everything I could so that she could also study. Quotations concerning the prenatal period seemed to be going well. And in the first days of the birth of my son, when exactly I was giving the first chocolate cigars to my director, she was thanking me for having worked until that last day in her institution.

What was happening?!

On the other hand. The weeks passed and happiness made us stronger. Ready to do better things. Although two months later, my son's health seemed to show signs of something unexpected. And so, we find it. The great respect I have for having enjoyed my son's life together for 4 beautiful months strongly shook my spirit.

I entered to teach English at the elementary level at the school where my first daughter attended. All right. We were together. And, as the assistant to the director, the mother of my children did her social service. Congratulations, shortly after she was titled.

I had to make something happen to improve my situation and that of my family. To make this great panorama of the accomplishment of what many believe impossible. Making the impossible possible.

From all this experience I noticed an old and negative behavior deeply rooted in people. Those who first judge your qualities, immediately, the richness of your speech to appropriate it, without proposing anything, and then, suggesting your ideas as theirs, are showing excessive and harmful signs of negativity.

They do not know that any business to be successful will be based on a certain number of specific qualities to be developed towards all levels of action. Something I have always known, but I had to finish figuring out perfectly.

To do this, you must first recognize your lack of learning and you should not be ashamed of it, because all those moments are what lead you to greatness. The same ones that have led me to glimpse the fantastic combination in which businesses work, in this one, the principle that I want you to forge as the Tequila Sunrise for Business, and that I will continue narrating to you later, remembering what, since I am an infant, I have felt inside me to the certainty:

Succeeding is to combine your intelligence and enthusiasm. If all you have left is just get up, take them and get what you are passionate about.

Business background
Breaking the ice

Don't let the fear of losing be greater than the excitement of winning
ROBERT KIYOSAKI
American investor, businessman, self-help author, motivational speaker and
financial literacy activist

Large transnational companies have been characterized as highly successful organisms, especially with regard to joint dominance of the three key ingredients that make consumer appeal in the international market. Nonetheless, to stay connected to the commercial system and immersed in the current globalization phenomenon and which it is almost impossible be isolated, are required to enter quickly and efficiently the strategies to ensure the true differential force that triggers win in business and apply them correctly as seen in commercial firms with high levels of development.

Part of this is shown by a study of Bruce, Cooper, & Vazquez (1999) applied to small businesses in the United Kingdom in which their results suggest that small businesses need to increase their interest in the design and incorporate it as an important process on their companies, including companies that took advantage of the design and they appreciated as a beneficial element for success of their projects. The study notes that one of the main causes of failure of design in this type of companies is the lack of interest and commitment that entrepreneurs show towards design.

Similarly, Iduarte & Zarza (2004) studied how the Micro, Small and Medium Enterprises (MSMEs) in the state of Estado de Mexico make use of professional design services, they consider that knows the methods of administering it and know how to apply on these segment of businesses, increase knowledge of designers about how is that micro, small and medium entrepreneurs manage and take advantage of design. They indicate that despite the fact that the design is considered as a very important element, it is clear that there is a low design understanding and commitment by managers and that a high percentage of design projects is done by themselves or are in charge their friends and acquaintances.

The study suggests that entrepreneurs see design as an external process, cheaper, and for occasional acquisition, rather than perceiving it as a necessary and integrated business process in the company.

Is worth mentioning that although a large percentage of employers indicated that the contracted designers showed a passive attitude, misunderstanding the requirements and business conditions, constant delays in the process and lack of experience, refer that the effective use of design can contribute positively to the differentiation and functioning of the company. However, the authors claim that small businesses are often unaware of the business impact that can generate investment in design.

Likewise, in a study conducted by Guijosa & Frías (2006) to a sample of 253 consumers of different social classes residents of Mexico City and the Estado de Mexico, was sought if the tangible product attributes are important as part of the intent at the time making the purchase. Secondly identify whether additionally, consumers have in mind or consider at the time of purchase subjective aspects of symbolic type.

Regarding the first raised specific objective, evidence was found indicating that the design is conceived as a set of tangible attributes related to a sense of belonging and self-satisfaction and influences purchasing choices of an individual is found so that their preference lean toward for the "aesthetic looks" of a product but the need variable is in between because your choice is limited by the quality.

The results of the second objective of the study founded indicate that buying motives have to do with a line of reasoning value for money, based on subjective aspects; a symbolic added value of emotional affective nature, through stimuli, feelings and symbolism that design communicates.

Also, Google in December 2011 published online the "ZMOT e-book: Winning the Zero Moment of Truth," which showed the new mental model now proposed by the consumer.

In this paper, global CEO of Saatchi & Saatchi X, Dina Howell says, "We recently conducted a study to understand the emotional benefits that drive and influence shopping behavior. Those benefits, we found, include the satisfaction of deep needs for self-creation, mastery, security and connection. Shoppers today want to explore and think about how products can improve their lives. They do reconnaissance to gain the insights they need, and they're driven to bond with others and enrich relationships as they learn. They are motivated by a desire to take charge of their own identities and the well-being of their families and homes."

The study suggests that there is now another crucial moment of decision that happens before consumers get to the store. No matter what you sell, customers will be carried first impression of a product, and quite possibly will make the final decision on the Zero Moment of Truth (ZMOT): 24/7 global consumer interaction that allows companies win the day.

Selecting the best ice cubes

The biggest adventure you can ever take is to live the life of your dreams
OPHRA WINFREY
American media executive, actress, talk show host, television producer, and philanthropist

The above studies suggest on the one hand, that the benefits that design can bring their companies are unknown, on the other, that is managed with mismanagement by omitting the integration of design as an internal process of the company and finally, a higher and more accurate focus is required in the use of marketing to satisfy the aesthetic and emotional benefits consumers looking. Disciplines to be properly taken as advantage can ensure the proper execution of the project, adequate market acceptance and efficiency in the functioning of the company.

In sum, there has been a phenomenon in the critical moment of purchase decision, in which to focus efforts mentioned can lead to consumer participation endorsement, that it is vital now to win in business.

If we observe the business landscape, situating us within like generators and from outside as their end consumers, supported by indicators of previous studies, there may be enough evidence pointing to a lack of attention and knowledge:

First, among MSMEs towards the three disciplines, that act as the main pillars of business, that well developed jointly can define the aggrandizement of a company and generate better products that satisfy the changing demands of the market.

Then, the emergence of a new purchasing model based on the information sharing consumers about the best products, which largely determines a new moment in the process, where the buyer needs are satisfied, that will influence the success or failure of most brands in the world.

Adding the needed ice cubes

It's fine to celebrate success, but it is more important to heed the lessons of
failure
BILL GATES
American business magnate, software developer, investor, and philanthropist

Business with this recipe requiring the correct dose of ice, which contributes greatly with the required objective to comply in business, achieve success.

The ice here complements the Tequila Sunrise for Business, than in this case it is necessary to stimulate you to get what you want to achieve, so that you have real bases and that observe how it is possible correctly project yourself to success with a business project, it is the testimony of 9 of the world's richest entrepreneurs.

This testimonies as success stories, shows and have sufficient elements to consider them as a reference, because each of these, fits perfectly with the development of the cocktail ingredients, that is, Tequila, Orange, and Grenadine, by which corresponds to the development of business in general, in the great diversity of their successful movements; as regards the work of each advice in particular, which together as a whole collaborate to build the Sunrise in a company. And I know that they, will express the best experience as part of the fantasy Tequila Sunrise, I have chosen for you. Ice whose name: With 9 of the most amazing experiences of the world's billionaires to build portentous foundations. The testimonies of billionaires presented here, are part of the best ice cubes selected that make the glass resonate and showing the mettle of the Tequila Sunrise for Business.

Echoing the right tumbler

On holding your ground: Stand by your principles and be comfortable with
confrontation
TRAVIS KALANICK
American billionaire businessman and co-founder

The Tequila Sunrise is a sample of the fundamentals that move big business in the commercial system in which we live. And also, it is the reflection of the principles with which the energy that sustains nature moves. Therefore, it describes the way in which the creative force has been developed by nature in society to be applied to the company, marketing, and consumption with the aim of correctly forming a business that can be projected at the level you want to reach.

Since business is the system that we all recognize to obtain the livelihoods and because the dominant business levels use them to thrive and achieve success, it is pressing to know how businesses develop in order not only to survive but to dominate the business system and continue to contribute better to the development of our society.

Talking about energy in business is because everything in the universe is energy and energy in general has three forces: positive, neutral, and negative, that is why it is triune; this energy by its nature is expressed to create; we, being immersed in business direct it as a projection mental to form the trading system, and for businesses to function properly we have to put their triune quality into action correctly. So, to be able to handle that creative mental projection, you have to confer on it: The negative energy, the orderly construction of a portent.

The neutral energy, the expansive malleability of passion. And the positive energy, the generation of evidence of desire. To thus enter business.

It is the best way to conduct energy by developing it in business to achieve well-being.

By correctly adding these ingredients, the energy, when constituting its triune completeness seeks harmony by random impulses of creation to continually maintain order (-), achieve further expansion (n), and leave new evidence (+), adapting it in the best way to any situation.

The Tequila Sunrise is the way that the energy of life is expressed everywhere in front of your eyes as irreplaceable forces and ingredients, which are encrypted because they maintain the natural code of the universe to create reality. And, it is for Business because I want you to understand how it has been put into operation in the commercial system so that you can adopt it and be successful in it.

Therefore, Tequila Sunrise for Business wants to be the open gap that illuminates your vision so that you can lean on the force of creation with the intention of changing the paradigm of not being able to have your own or successful business and eradicate the implanted programming of obstacles and scarce with which you live, to establish that of fluidity and abundance through the combination of three key ingredients to take your business to the level you want to achieve.

The base with which businesses move and that you are going to learn is scrupulous, therefore, it will need your greatest concentration so that you can understand that after knowing it you have to take it to action with all your strength with that business that can generate abundance in your organization, a positive impact on the market and a genuine change in the lives of others.

Placed the containers on the bar

I knew that if I failed, I wouldn't regret that, but I knew the one thing I might regret is not trying
JEFF BEZOS
American founder & CEO

The projects do not walk alone, they need your intent and your desire to finally materialize.

By this I mean if you really want to achieve success, you are leaving a possibility as a tendency to exist in reality. If you are very specific in how you want it and you work hard to get what you need, in a few words, you are gathering the energy necessary for it possibility to project in your reality, and therefore you are opening a vortex, which will accommodate the accumulation of energy that you have generated, ordering as you have arranged to detonate with the same force that you wanted to make it come true, a reality that is waiting for you.

Therefore, choose well what you really want, objective to which you will drive full force of your intention, and will download the best of you if you know give the right frequency to each ingredient to achieve business you expect. If you do, that you really want will result of this and will accommodate to your request to harmonize with you.

Select well your collaborators, your representative segment, and your target market; to find your faithful consumer correctly. That is, choose well ice you need, they represent the same intention that want to take as a result.

Once you have ready on the bar the elements you need, both the tumbler will receive the prepare, as the ice cubes will give vigor to this, then poured one by one the ingredients that you have developed in your business and gives its qualities to your firm, your brand, and your services or products. The pouring of the ingredients will take strength, flavor, and consistency upon contact with ice cubes that you chose and combine each and every one of them. It will endow its effects to your end consumer, if you know anticipate with the Tequila Sunrise based on what they want and at the times requires it. Adjust the correct doses will be given you, until achieving a cocktail at his point.

I truly hope that through the Tequila Sunrise for Business you get the reality you want.

Serving the Tequila on business
Administration

Management is efficiency in climbing the ladder of success; leadership determines whether the ladder is leaning against the right wall
STEPHEN COVEY
American educator, author, businessman, and keynote speaker

As the first ingredient of the Tequila Sunrise for Business, its function is to form the structure by which the conduct of your business will build. Its main task, is to provide the active substance shall grant presence to the objectives of your company, in order to maintain direction in your business and its effects on your audience.

According Chiavenato (2001) the word administration comes from the Latin *ad* (management, trend) and *minister* (subordination or obedience) meaning, fulfillment of a function under the command of another, namely, providing a service to another. However, the original meaning of this word has undergone a radical transformation.

The administration, as we know it today, is the historical outcome and integrated cumulative contribution of many pioneers, philosophers, physicists, economists, statisticians and even entrepreneurs that over time were developing and disseminating works and theories in their field activities. It is therefore not surprising that widely use certain modern management concepts and principles discovered in the mathematical sciences, as statistics; the human sciences such as psychology, sociology, education or biology; in the physical sciences like physics or chemistry; as well as law and engineering among others.

On the way emerged important management theories that have their main approaches and each one favors a variable that emphasizes the point of view from which it develops. Although by itself the content of management study varies widely by theory or school considered, somehow all administrative theories are applicable to current situations to be used in each context, therefore management has become one of the most significant human activity areas.

Despite all the progress made by human knowledge, the called management science flourished just in the early twentieth century, and it was a historical event of significance.

The administration is an important activity in a pluralistic society based on cooperation activities that people develop in organizations. From the moment in which organizations reached a certain size and complexity, administration began to present difficulties and challenges hitherto ignored by managers, who needed new administrative developments.

This process is ongoing and requires a set of people in different hierarchical levels that deal with different issues, therefore management has become one of the most important areas of human activity. By living in a civilization where the cooperative effort of the people is the fundamental base of society, the administration is essential to the existence, survival and success of organizations.

Hence arose the growing need to develop a theory of management that allowed offer managers of organizations suitable models and strategies to solve their business problems.

In this regard it is important to know some definitions of management to enrich our landscape and understand the general meaning of discipline:

Taylor, mentioned in Chiavenato (2001) argues that the administration has emphasis on the tasks performed within a company when to focus attention on improving the effectiveness of the company is first required to meet the increased efficiency at the operational level.

To Fayol (as cited in Chiavenato 2001), the administration is an applied social science that studies the organizations responsible for planning, organizing, directing, coordinating and controlling the resources of an organization (human, financial, material, technological, intellectual, and so on) in order to obtain the maximum possible economic or social benefit, according to its objectives, in which the company start of a synthetic, global and universal approach that begins with its anatomical and structural conception as an organization. For him, administration is a whole of which the organization is one of the parts, and only refers to the establishment of the structure and form, so it is static and limited. La organización formal se basa en la división del trabajo racional, está planeada en el papel, explicada, descrita con reglas, procedimientos y cargos. The informal organization appears spontaneously among friends and groups of antagonism without appearing on a chart, or any other formal document.

According to Kaplan (2014) the administration is an intercultural and social management based on an interdisciplinary approach.

García Padilla (2014) said that, since modern management of an organization is centered on strategy and focused on customer needs, it is possible to conceive of administration, such as management developed human talent to facilitate the work of a group workers within an organization. In order to meet overall goals, both institutional and personal, regularly goes hand in hand with the application of techniques and principles of the administrative process, where the leading role is optimal and efficient development, creating certainty in the conduct of the people and the application of different resources.

Basic concept: The management process is the result of the basic activity of collaboration towards a common goal, which is manifested by the concepts of organization and strategy aimed at business.

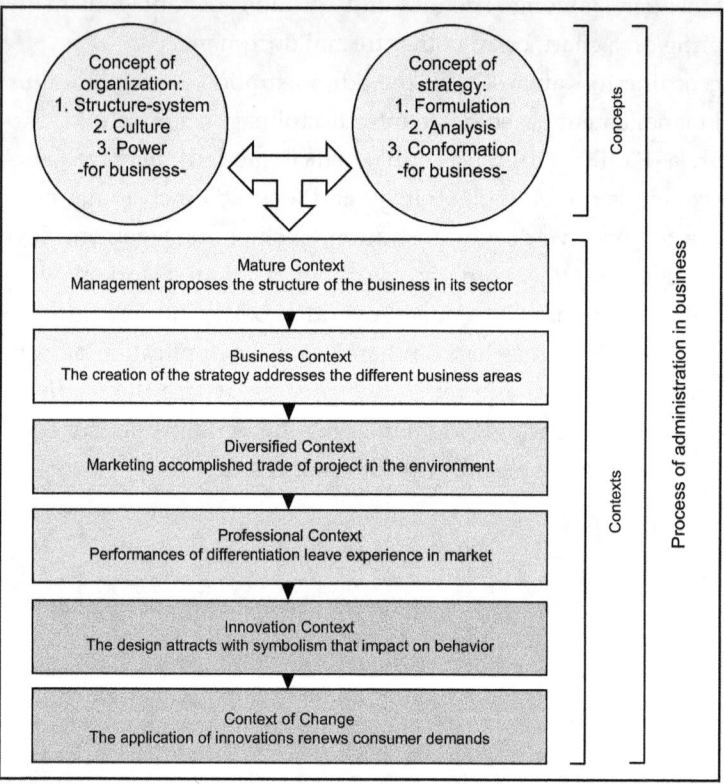

The administration process in business. Adapted from: Mintzberg, Henry; J. Brian; J. Voyer. *El proceso estratégico. Conceptos, contextos y casos.* [The strategic process. Concepts, contexts and cases]. Mexico: Prentice Hall Hispano-American, 1997. 641 pp. intro.

Administration and business

An organization without human commitment is like a person without a soul
HENRY MINTZBERG
Internationally recognized Canadian academic and author on business

According to Chiavenato (2001) The General Administrative Theory (GAT) is the field of knowledge that deals with the study of administration in general and of all organizations. The chronology of the main events of the origins of the administration towards its subject matter has evolved since the beginning of civilization:

• 4000 B.C. The Egyptians recognized the need to plan, organize and control.

• 2600 B.C. Decentralize the organization.

• 2000 B.C. Recognize the written orders and consulting.

• 1800 B.C. Hammurabi uses the written control sets the minimum wage and acknowledges that responsibility cannot be transferred.

• 1491 B.C. The Hebrew achieves organizational concepts, scale and exception.

• 600 B.C. Nebuchadnezzar controls production and wage incentives.

• 500 B.C. Mencius in China recognizes the need for standard systems.

• 400 B.C. Cyrus in Persia and Socrates in Greece forth the universality of management and Plato the principle of specialization.

• 175 B.C. Cato in Rome uses the description of functions.

• 284. Diocletian delegates authority.

• 1436. Arsenal of Venice makes cost accounting, checks and balances to control inventory numbers, assembly line and staff management.

• 1525. Machiavelli begins consensus, cohesion and leadership.

• 1767. Sir James Stuart creates the source of authority, differentiation of hierarchies based on the advantages of specialization.

• 1776. Adam Smith in England begins specialization of workers and the concept of control with the use of the steam engine and its application to production during the Industrial Revolution.

- 1799. Eli Whitney in the United States employs quality control and recognizes the administrative amplitude.
- 1800. James Watt and Matthew Boulton in England standardized production, working methods, times, specifications, gives benefits and uses the audit.
- 1810. Robert Owen applied practices and training to employees and gives house plans.
- 1832. Charles Babbage emphasizes specialization, division of labor, time, motion and color effects on the efficiency of the labor applied in uniform and announcements.
- 1856. Daniel C. McCallum in the United States uses the chart to show the organizational structure.
- 1886. Henry Metcalfe employed the administration as art and science.
- Since 1900, begins The General Administrative Theory with industrial pioneers and entrepreneurs from big companies like General Electric, Singer, Rockefeller, Westinghouse, Ford, and so on. And it is Frederick W. Taylor who made possible by activating the evolution of what we now know as business management:
- In 1903 with scientific management using cooperation needs between workers and management, salary increases, exception principle applied to the production floor, study methods, time study, and emphasis on research, planning and control.
- It was followed in 1909 the theory of bureaucracy: With the emphasis on peaceful behavior of the internal elements of the company.
- After 1916 the classical theory by Henry Fayol: Emphasized in managing the main direction and subordination.
- In 1932 the theory of human relations: In an effort to decide all people in the organization.
- In 1947 structuralist theory: Concentrated in the intra-organizational analysis and business departments.
- In 1951 the systems theory: Giving full importance to the environment surrounding the company towards a socio-technical approach.
- In 1954 neoclassical theory: Highlighting the general principles of management and administrator functions.

- In 1957 behavioral theory: Emphasizing the styles of management and integration of individual decisions.
- In 1962 the theory of organizational development: Committed to organizational change planned for the growth of the company.
- By 1972 the situational theory focused on changes affecting the company with an environmental imperative and use of technology.
- And then the contingency theory: With the emphasis on how best to adapt to external changes with the use of technology.

In outlining the gradual steps of administration, the effect of the various theories with their contributions and valid points for any organization or company is shown. Although each theory arose as a response to business problems of his time, all administrative theories are applicable to current situations in business.

In that sense, Wikipedia.org (2015) says that a business is to create or constitute an entity with a system, method or manner in order to get money for production activities (as does a factory), marketing (as does a store or a distributor) or services (as does an establishment or a workshop), that benefit others.

To start a business, you need to develop a business model, this is understood as the type of activity to do with strategy, or planting of the factors or elements that make up the business. So, the commercial or social activity that has been thought and that is to be developed is the core business. And formed a tool that allows us to organize and planning activities that must be performed to achieve the goals of our company cooperatively.

A well-run business must have a store displaying their products or services, to invite do different payment transactions. It consists of professionally perform the activities from production and beyond sales, personnel distributed at different hierarchical levels clearly defined responsibilities.

Basic concept: The active and productive life of companies only guarantees for those them to reach a sound understanding of its strategic responsibilities, disciplines that underpin and maturity of its business basic model. (Adapted from Colmenares, 1992, Intro.)

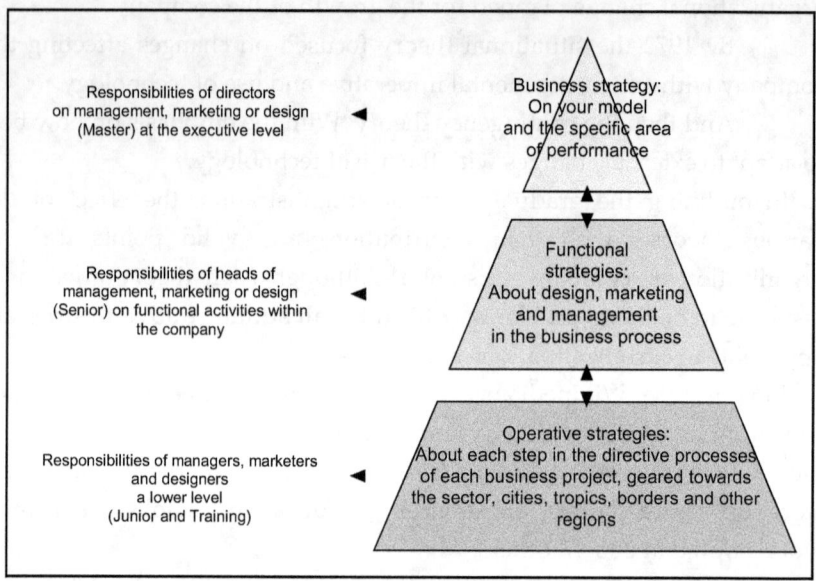

The Pyramid of the creation of the strategy in a company of single business. Adapted from: Thompson, Arthur; Strickland, A. J. *Strategic management. Concepts and cases*. USA: Mc Graw Hill, 2004. 398 pp. p. 53.

The purpose of administration

Whenever you see a successful business, someone once made a courageous decision
PETER DRUKER
Austrian-born, American management consultant, educator, and author

To Chiavenato (2001) the world today is a society composite of organizations oriented to production of goods or "products" and the provision of specialized activities or "services," which are planned, coordinated, directed and controlled in organizations, which are constituted by individuals and non-human resources. The lives of people dependent organizations and the latter depend on the work of the former. Some organizations are called corporations, whether or not for profit.

In any form of human endeavor, the efficiency with which people work together to achieve common goals depends primarily on the ability of those who exercise administrative functions, this function is performed in each discipline within an organization.

Each company should be considered from the point of view of the effectiveness and efficiency simultaneously.

1. Effectiveness is a measure of achievement of results.
2. Efficiency is a measure of resource utilization in the process.

Although the recent administrative theory has shifted the focus of "a better way," endeavor to achieve the best project without determining the correct strategy, towards the approach of "everything depends on," or achieving a good strategy and adapt to the context depending on the market movements; every organization needs to be managed in an appropriate way to achieve their goals more efficiently and effectively. The ideal would be an efficient and effective company, which constitute excellence.

Nowadays the administration, studies companies and other types of organizations, from the point of view of interaction and interdependence among six main variables:

1. People: the skills of business professionals.
2. Environment: developing business industry chosen.

3.	Tasks: the administrative process in every area of business.

4.	Structure: the distribution of responsibilities within the company.

5.	Technology: the tools and the most appropriate means.

6.	Competitiveness: Tactical differentiator, contact and visual.

Each which is specific object of study by the administrative theory and are essential components in the study of business administration.

The behavior of these components is systemic and complex because each one influence and is influenced by other components. The changes that take place in one cause changes greater or lesser degree in others. Overall behavior is different from the sum of the behavior of each component considered separately. The new variable, competitiveness, complements each and every one of the above variables; it incorporates the necessary push to mobilize that complex whole in the pursuit of excellence, thus avoiding the compliance.

Due to the increasing importance of management and new and complex challenges it faces, the balance is variously inclined to certain individual aspects of the enormous context of variables involved in the structure and behavior of organizations.

In the coming decades, major management challenges will:

1.	Growth of organizations: Successful organizations tend to the growth and expansion of its activities, either in terms of size and resources, expand their markets or the size of their operations.

2.	Fierce competition: As more markets and business, so do the risks in business. The product or service that proves to be superior or better will be the one with higher demand.

3.	Sophistication of technology: With the progress of communications, computer, and transport, organizations and companies have internationalized their operations and activities.

4.	High inflation rates: The costs of energy, raw materials, labor force and money are continually rising. Inflation requires increasingly greater efficiency in business so they can get better results with the available resources and reducing operating costs.

5.	Economic globalization and internationalization of business: Export activity and the creation of new subsidiaries in foreign territories are a recent phenomenon, which will influence the future organization and management. Competition becomes worldwide due to global trade.

6. Greater role of organizations: As they grow, organizations become more competitive, technologically sophisticated, and more international and, with this, increase its environmental impact.

The major management challenges related to adapt and integrate the six variables mentioned.

In this regard, Chiavenato notes that the adequacy and integration among these six variables are the main management challenges. And also mentions that as the administration is facing new situations that arise over time and space, administrative doctrines and theories need to adapt their approaches or modify them to remain useful and applicable. This explains, in part, the gradual steps from the General Theory of Administration, over time, and the breadth and complexity gradual.

The basic task of management is to carry out activities in an orderly manner with the participation of all people immersed in that process, interpret the objectives proposed by an organization and transform them into teamwork through planning, organizing, the direction and control of all activities in their areas and levels, in order to achieve those objectives in the most appropriate manner to the situation.

So, that Mintzberg, Brian, & Voyer (1997) say that the structure of the overall strategy must reflect the situation of the organization:

1. Their age.
2. Size or number of members.
3. The type of production system or tasks.
4. The degree of complexity and dynamism of technology and its environment.

They mention that, as some organizations have cultures underdeveloped or cultures that are not distinctive at all and these organizations with weak cultures can be considered unsuccessful in stylistic terms.

And moreover, as companies with strong cultures, by coincidence or by design, can be considered rich in stylistic terms, whose members identify with the organization and committed to values and beliefs that are inspirational, where these values contribute to the stability of the organization and are an instrument used to the new members to understand the events and activities that occur in there.

Organizational culture is important to understand a number of intangible elements that are shared by members of an organization; their values, beliefs that guide their actions, innuendoes, and even how to think.

Therefore, we must skillfully address the two levels on which occurs normally organizational culture:

The observable level such as clothing people behavior and material environment.

As the deep level that represents the true culture and rituals, ceremonies, stories, symbols and language.

As the basics of culture and organizational strategy that will help fulfill the purpose of the administration.

Basic concept: All variables of an organization are directed to productive teamwork, they maintain interdependence in all senses for proper interaction between their activities.

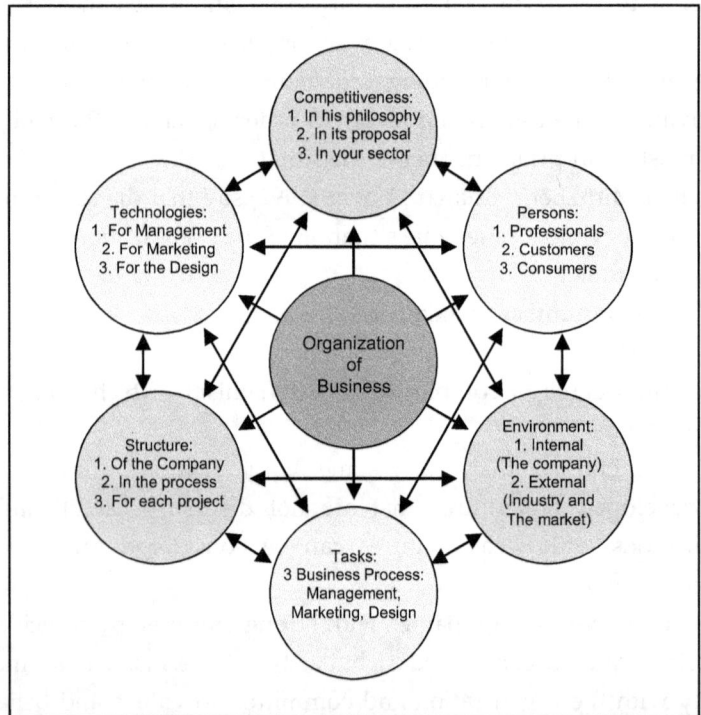

Basic variables of management within an organization. Adapted from: Chiavenato, Idalberto. *Introducción a la teoría general de la administración*. [Introduction to general management theory]. Mexico: McGraw-Hill, 2001. 1056 pp. p. 14.

The strategic direction of management

Chiavenato (2001) indicates that administration arises from the conception that every business can be divided into six groups called the basic management functions:

1.   Technical Functions: related to the production of goods and services of the company.

2.   Commercial Functions: related to the purchase, sale and exchange.

3.   Financial Functions: related to the search and management of capital.

4.   Safety Features: relating to the protection and preservation of goods and people.

5.   Accounting Functions: related to inventories, records, balances, costs and statistics.

6.   Administrative Functions: related to the integration of the other five functions of management. Administrative functions coordinate and synchronize the other functions of the company and are always above them.

These latter functions, administrative, thus defining the act of managing according Fayol (in Chiavenato 2001) and containing the universal functions of management who are the called administrative process are present in any activity manager at any level or area of activity of the company:

1.   Planning: visualize the future and chart a program of action.

2.   Organizing: building the physical and social structures of the company.

3.   Directing: guiding and orienting staff.

4.   Coordinating: link, unite and harmonize all acts and collective efforts.

5.   Controlling: check that everything happens according to established rules and orders given.

Any member of a company performs these functions by participating in these guidelines from any level.

Hil & Jones (2005) explain that to correctly carry these administrative functions throughout the organization should focus attention on the strategic process, it analyzes all the functions of a company defines its action through appropriate strategies and headed inside and outside the company in order to get the best results.

In this manner, administration introduces the concept of situational analysis refers to analyzing the internal and external environment in which the analysis of the position of the company is made. This analysis involves a combination of strengths, weaknesses, threats and opportunities facing a business.

The strategic management process consists of five components:

1.   The selection of the mission and major corporate goals.

2.   The analysis of the external differentiation environment of the organization to identify *Opportunities and Threats.*

3.   Analysis of the internal operating environment of the organization, which highlights its *Strengths and Weaknesses.*

4.   The selection of strategies based on the *strengths* of the organization and corrects their *weaknesses* in order to take advantage of external *opportunities* and to counter external *threats.*

5.   The implementation of the strategy. The company expects the implementation of its resources by way of achieving your goals and accomplish adapt as best as possible to their environment.

Analyze the environments is called strategy formulation. The implementation of strategies involves the settings on organizational structures and control systems to put into action the strategy. This analysis is known as (SWOT) *Strengths, Weaknesses, Opportunities and Threats.*

Under this scenario as Thompson & Strickland (1998) we see that the SWOT analysis forms a matrix that is transcendental for organizations.

In its first phase are those that form part of the internal environment and indicate the variables on which the company can take action.

1.   The strengths; that are positive, including: • Fundamental capabilities in key areas • Adequate financial resources • Good image buyers • A recognized leader in the market • Strategies well designed functional areas • Access to economies of scale • Isolated (at least to

some degree) of strong competitive pressures • Technology ownership • Cost advantages • Best advertising campaigns • Skills for product innovation • Management able • Advantageous position in the experience curve • Best manufacturing capacity • Superior technological skills.

2.   The weaknesses; they are negative, such as: • No clear strategic direction • Obsolete facilities • Lower profitability average • Lack of opportunity and talent management • Poor monitoring in implementing the strategy • Abundance of internal operational problems • Delay in research and development • Line products too limited • Weak market image • Weak distribution network • Skills marketing below • Inability to finance the necessary changes in strategy • Higher general unit costs in relation to key competitors.

In its second phase are those forming part of the external environment and are factors which cannot be modified by the will of the company.

3.   The threats; they are negative, as: • Entry of foreign competitors with lower costs • Increased sales and substitute products • Slower growth in the market • Adverse changes in exchange rates and trade policies of foreign governments • Costly regulatory requirements • Vulnerability recession and business cycle • Increased bargaining power of customers or suppliers • Change in the needs and tastes of buyers • Adverse demographic changes.

4.   And the opportunities; that are positive, such as: • Addressing additional customer groups • Entering new markets or segments • Expand the product line to satisfy a wider range of customer needs • Diversifying into related products • Vertical integration (forward or backward) • Removing trade barriers in foreign markets attractive • Complacency among the rival companies • Fastest growth in the market.

The administrator must identify the factors on which work hard, first to remove those within the category of risky and secondly to protect and enrich those who favor him.

Basic Concept: The strategic management process raises the mission statement of the company tends to focus on their business perspective (who we are and what we do) generally describes the capabilities of the company, its strategic approach and the current appearance their businesses.

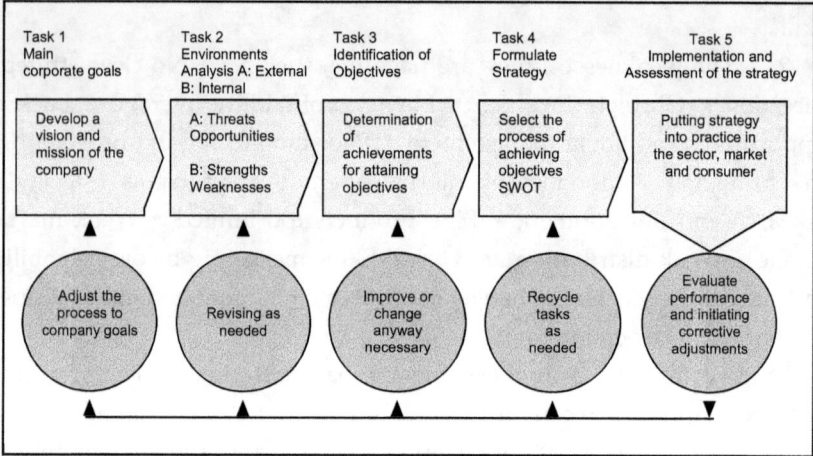

The five tasks of strategic management. Adapted from: Thompson, Arthur; Strickland, A. J. *Strategic management. Concepts and cases.* USA: Mc Graw Hill, 2004. 398pp. p. 7. And: Hill, Charles W. L.; Jones, Gareth R. *Administración estratégica. Un enfoque integrado.* [Strategic management. An integrated approach]. Mexico: McGraw-Hill Interamericana, 2005. 915 pp. p. 10.

The business plan

Thinking out a plan and ensuring its success is one of the keenest satisfactions for an intelligent man to experience
HENRY FAYOL
French engineer and director of mines, theoretical of business administration

When starting your business project can easily happen to forget the business plan, considering that to have found a need in the market and provide a product or service, necessarily will succeed. However, if there is no strong planning, it is certainly will not sustain growth.

Make a business plan raises the possibility succeed and grow. Develop a strategy means knowing the map indicating where you will take your project and you must start from a SWOT analysis already mentioned to capture it in a document called a business plan.

According to *Comisión Nacional para la Protección y Defensa de los Usuarios de Servicios Financieros (Condusef)* [National Commission for the Protection and Defense of Users of Financial Services] (2013) business plan is a guidance document for the employer whereby, processed, define and evaluate aspects that make up the idea or project business. This document is for the entrepreneur who seeks to realize his idea for the business when you want to define your project and for investors seeking to convince always new candidates to participate as partners in business.

Develop a business plan in a document allows the observation of likely future scenarios and variables, in order to facilitate a comprehensive analysis when seating the final position chosen. Allows imagine ideas, solutions and results, to be clear how to turn them into reality. It's also a map that can be presented to other parties involved in the project as investors, partners, banks, suppliers and customers.

The advantages of a business plan are varied, marks the moment in the life of the company and the type or business model to be planned. Ensures a business has operational and financial sense, prior to commissioning. Seek the most efficient way of carrying out a project. Create a panorama that identifies needs, avoid obstacles and allocate resources previously to the fact, taking leads to savings in time, money and effort. Evaluate the performance having an ongoing business. Help make improvements to business processes. It is a guide to correct the path and cause changes to the business.

Develop a business plan allows to establish a significant and necessary distance between changes unfounded (occurrences) and business decisions foundation (planning) taken based on the information and analysis.

The process to be followed to make a business plan varies according to each company, but in general it is advisable to consider the following points:

Mature or specify the business idea to perform. Organize all the information available to capture aspects that affect business operations, review what information is missing and get it. Assess if you can do it yourself, or require the participation of other individuals or teams and external professionals, area managers, employees, and so on.

For Berry (2014) all movement of the company is important to have a plan. So, to know where you're going, you need to know where you come from and what path you traveled. Here are some general elements of a successful business plan.

1.   Description of Business. You must define various aspects of your offer as the context of your industry, service address, and the purpose of your contribution, your business goals and general objectives in the short, medium and long term. This section is the backbone of your business plan and prepares the stage for the rest of the information.

2.   Products and services. All have a product or service that is aimed at a target audience. You must be able to describe what you sell and identify what makes your product unique.

3.   Sales and marketing. This section opens the window industry, market conditions, general costs and gives you the opportunity to distinguish yourself from the competition. Describe how you see your merchandise and branding to be recognized at scales from the personal to the global.

4.   Operations. The purpose of this aspect is to help highlight the administrative side of your business, including how you move, the location of your office, equipment management, public relations, network providers, and so on.

5.   Human talent. One that is, if you have consultants, partners, directors or people to help in your business, this is where you understand their involvement and ability to contribute to your success. If there is a hierarchy of positions within your company and the relevance of each relationship.

6.   Development. The part where you can imagine the visionary management. Not everything in this section is based on the facts as the information itself you bring in the other sections. Here you project into the future and think big. The development is an important part of the business to continue differentiating you, you should be sure to complete these visions to land them into goals.

7.   Financial Summary. Where composing a history of your investments, financial dealings and how you managed to get the position you have now. With some flexibility, you'll understand how to operate your business; you'll see your financial statement, including how the numbers are balanced at the end of each month, the health of your business and cash flow.

8.   Executive Summary. It is a composition of one or two pages of your business plan. It is best done when you finished all the details of the plan.

According Myownbusiness.org (2013) the main value of the business plan is to create the project in writing that evaluates all aspects of the viability of the business venture describing and analyzing business expectations. The preparation and maintenance of a business plan is important for any industry regardless of size or money. But does not guarantee success. If not properly value their potential, then the business plan could become a guide to failure. If a proper assessment of the economic changes of business is maintained, the plan will not only be a useful guide but also a financial tool for success.

This is an essential step you should take as a prudent businessman, regardless of the size of your business.

ARTIUX

1.	DESCRIPTION OF BUSINESS:
2.	NICHE MARKETS:
3.	TERRITORIES OR GEOGRAPHICAL COVERAGE OF BUSINESS:
4.	DESIRED POSITIONING:
5.	BUSINESS UNIQUE PROPOSAL:
6.	BASIC INVESTMENT TO DEVELOP THE BUSINESS:
Identify the amount to invest to start the business, as well as the origin or source and the conditions of financial resources (contributions, loan, society, and so on).	
7.	FINANCIAL GOALS:
In 3 months; in 6 months; 12 months; 24 months; 36 months.	
8.	TYPE AND NUMBER OF UNITS SOLD:
Products; Services; Packages; (Include quantity to sell and date must achieve the target) Name; Product Type; Existing develop; Estimated selling units Quantity; Estimated Sales Price; Scheduled date for achieving the goal sales.	
9.	PRICES:
10.	MEANS OF MARKETING FOR THESE NICHES:
11.	GOALS OF MARKETING: (development of marketing tools and applications to achieve the above sales).
Identifying the stages of development and compliance required to have a means of marketing complete and ready for use in business.	
Medium; Components; Description; Start; End; Expected product.	
12.	GOALS FOR DEVELOPMENT OF NEW PRODUCTS; Services; Packages; Product Type; Name; Start; End; (repeated for each different product).
13.	PROMOTIONAL MATERIALS:

Format of basic business plan. Adapted from: *Nacional Financiera (Nafin)* [National Financer] (2009). *13 pasos para hacer tu plan de negocios. Guía del participante.* [13 steps to make your business plan. Participant guide]. 32 pp. capacitación@nafin.gob.mx, www.nafin.gob.mx/portalnf/get?file=/pdf/otros/TRECE-PASOS.pdf

TEQUILA SUNRISE FOR BUSINESS

Basic Concept: The business plan is the tool that projects all activities of an organization regardless of size. Must be done from entrepreneurship and renewed according to changes in the lifetime of the company.

I.	ASPECTS OF MARKET AND MARKETING

1. Business detail. 2. Description of the product. 3. Description of services. 4. Specific objectives. 5. General objectives. 6. Philosophy. 7. Securities. 8. Mission. 9. Vision. 10. Market opportunities that give rise to the project. 11. Motivation. 12. Profile whom it is directed. 13. Market research. 14. Economic density product. 15. Feasibility of business development. 16. Main clients. 17. Major competitors. 18. Major suppliers. 19. Timing of product on the market. 20. Geographical distribution. 21. Supply and demand. 22. Rates and prices. 23. Plus product. 24. Policies and sales strategies.

II.	TECHNICAL ASPECTS

1. Condition and operation of the project. 2. Location. 3. Reason for the location. 4. General Resources. 5. Permissions. 6. Appropriate size of the facility. 7. Architectural plan. 8. Effects of energy use. 9. Estimated ecological impact. 10. Wastewater discharge. 11. Organic waste. 12. Inorganic waste. 13. The availability and quality of raw materials. 14. Production capacity. 15. Product Requirements. 16. Quality Control. 17. Scope of strategic point. 18. Scope of point of differentiation. 19. Scope of point innovation. 20. Development of global communication. 21. Consistency of corporate identity and brand.

III.	ADMINISTRATIVE ASPECTS

1. Timing of activities: general description processes. 2. Schedule of activities: Duration of individual projects. 3. Strategic Conduct. 4. Management skills. 5. Professionalism of human talent. 6. Description of skilled labor. 7. Number of adequate staff. 8. Age of the organization. 9. Internal rules. 10. General Flowchart: Flow of the organizational structure. 11. Letter distribution of activities: Who does what and how much you earn. 12. Sustainability of the project: In what success is based. 13. Benefits. 14. Concerns. 15. State of the socio-economic environment in which the project is developed.

IV.	ECONOMIC-FINANCIAL ASPECTS

1. Budgets. 2. Investment. 3. Working capital. 4. Analysis WWISS: How I have to Work, Winning, and Investing, Saving, and Spending. 5. Statement. 6. Inflation. 7. Exchange. 8. Taxation. 9. Bank interest rate. 10. Convenience. 11. Recovery of invested capital. 12. Risk project. 13. Yields.

V.	SOCIAL ASPECTS

Benefit of project to society. 2. Direct effects. 3. Indirect Effects. 4. Magnitude of effects. 5. Sustainability of the project.

Format of business plan. Adapted from: *Nacional Financiera (Nafin)* [National Financer] (2002). capacitación@nafin.gob.mx

Strategy

A strategy delineates a territory in which a company seeks to be unique
MICHAEL PORTER
Professor at the Harvard Business School and global authority on strategy

Mintzberg et al., (1997) notes that the term strategy comes from the Greek *"strategos"* which means *"general."* In turn comes from roots meaning *"army"* and *"lead." Stratego* the Greek verb meaning "to plan the destruction of the enemy by reason of efficient use of resources."

The concept of strategy in a military and political context is well known for hundreds of years. In the case of modern competitive business with inclination to project strategies companies try to outperform their rivals.

To understand the role of business strategy, Mintzberg, discusses two approaches to the concept of strategy as distinguished as "School of design" and "School planning," mentions that the definitions of strategy that have been made since then are only changes in definitions of their authors Andrews and Ansoff respectively. And all these definitions have four things in common, so you might consider a uniform landscape of strategy in business.

The strategy from the point of view of the administration provides the next horizon:

1.   The environment: Internal and external, or own and outside company conditions to which you must respond. To implement business strategy in each process.

2.   The mission: A definition of the reason for existence of the company. To establish the true purpose of the company.

3.   The analysis of the situation: The processes to be performed to determine how pro their situation in the environments is. Be strengths or weaknesses (in the internal environment) or threats or opportunities (in the external environment).

4.   The application of resources: Towards the environment in which it competes. Resulting in the achievement of its objectives.

Therefore, the selection of a strategy should establish a position in the means in which it is developed and being this, a sector in business, market overview then arises.

So to Kotler & Armstrong (2003) establishing marketing strategy consists of the following components:

1.   Responding to the primary requirements of the company and observe the demands wake up in the market.

2.   Identify the competitive advantages on which to cement a position.

3.   Select the right and choose an overall business strategy for positioning.

4.   Communicate effectively and present the position chosen to market specifically to your target audience.

In this case each company should differentiate its offering by creating a unique package of competitive advantages.

From this perspective, when approached the target audience is that you can appreciate closely the strategy that requires the product, so it is possible to see the design.

The design strategy for (Zimmermann, 1998) and strategic process according to (idologie, 2012) consists of the following items:

1.   Analysis of the end or design / *LEVEL* design project. New product or service; *Renewal* of design; *Continuity* for line extension. By understanding, observation and definition of the type of project: Consulting, research and benchmarks for the first mental projection. *(R-C)*

2.   Analysis creative of design project / Current *ENVIRONMENT* image. Positioning: Current and central *Promise*, product *Perception*, raison d'être of the brand to the consumer; consumer: profile, SEL; category: competition and trends. Analyze what customers have in mind about the brand. For them their perception is reality. This perception must be sought directly in the market and not try to ask the staff or think like customers. *(P-P)*

3.   Analysis of means / Select product *STRATEGY*. Product vs. competition: Shared *Values*, points of contact of the category and *Qualities* shared within the category; functional and emotional attributes, performance differentiator own and inherited values; disadvantages vs. competition, weaknesses of the product and how to minimize. *(V-Q)*

4.   Strategy Action / *IMPLEMENTATION* design and objectives action. Desired positioning: How you want to be identified by the market, which will differ in order to achieve what you want, what quality will communicate; to the consumer: Retain current, adding new, changing consumer, profile and SEL of the new consumer; vs. competition, what should be the new *Personality* and tone of *Communication*, branding opportunities that the client detects, social or visual restrictions. Research and opinion. Viable strategy positioning: Premise: cannot be many things at the same time. Image strategy: Generate brand value and emotional bond. *(P-C)*

Strategic process that analyzes both the attributes won: Level and the Environment; as proposed attributes: Strategy and Implementation. So, I call (LESI) of the design project in its sphere of action.

Johnson, Whittington, & Scholes (cited by Free-management-ebooks.com, 2013) believe that "the strategy is the direction and scope of an organization over the long term, which achieves an advantage in an environmental change through its configuration of resources and expertise."

In general, Levy (1981) assures that the success of a company is the compatibility between environment and strategy. In this sense the strategic behavior entails adopting an appropriate strategic plan that includes goals, objectives and specific strategies:

1.   The long-term plan: Estimated exceeding five years.
2.   The medium-term plan: For periods between two and four years.
3.   The short-term plan: For periods of one to two years.

Although each organization will have differences in requirements can be formulated three basic criteria for determining the planning horizon:

1.   The accuracy of possible prediction of the chosen strategy.
2.   The nature of the products on the market.
3.   The commitment of the business model to future.

In this regard, Mintzberg (mentioned Hil & Jones, 2005) complements the administration intervenes when appropriate, discarding the bad strategies, whether these emerging (reactive adapted) or attempted (largely planned), but cultivating those potentially good.

However, Mintzberg et al., (1997) assert that "To make such decisions business managers must be able to judge the value of emerging strategies. Must be able to think strategically."

In general terms and for the build in your business, a strategy is a systematic series of actions planned in time, that are performed to accomplish a specific mission, which suits so well to benefit a company achieves differentiate uniquely.

Glimpsing the basic structure on which strategic thinking sits: competition.

Basic Concept: business administration must distinguish all kinds of strategies that are in part planned and reactive part, from its emergence and consider all your valuable components to achieve a better response to its purposes.

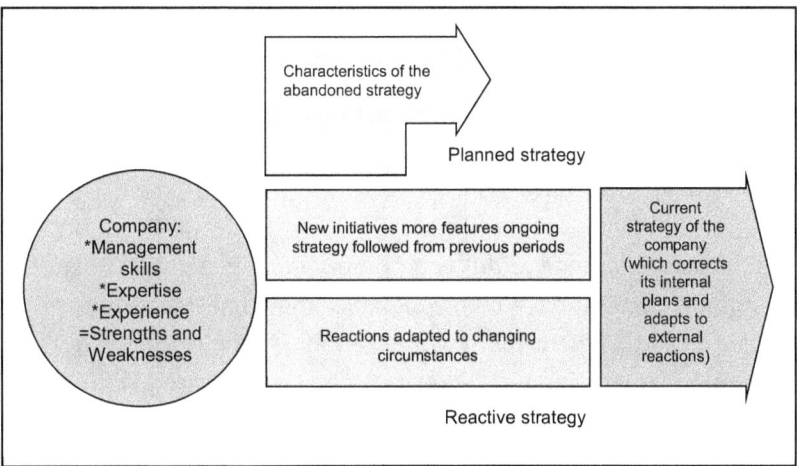

The strategy of a company. Adapted from: Thompson, Arthur; Strickland, A. J. *Strategic management. Concepts and cases*. USA: Mc Graw Hill, 2004. 398 pp. p. 12.

The ice on background | PART 1
Pervading Tequila

I am looking for a lot of men who have an infinite capacity to not know what can't be done
HENRY FORD
American industrial, founding and father of the modern production lines

---

CARLOS SLIM
Founder, president and counselor of Grupo Carso companies

Find the opportunities.

"It is already known and it is becoming more generalized that we are living a new civilization, a civilizational change that some thinkers called futurists began to perceive, such as Albin Tofler since the early 70s. Something that worried me. Unfortunately, I did not read Albin Tofler at that time, I met him already in the early 90's and I made a good friendship with him, and that was when I began to fully understand what was happening, what this new civilization means, the effects that it has, the challenges it causes, etc.

But before talking about this new civilization in which we are and in which we have to insert ourselves in the best way, some previous comments would be to show that this is the fourth stage of life for humanity. First, for more than two million years after origin, they say that in East Africa, our ancestors spent those two million years surviving, reproducing, and expanding so that, during that time of hunting and gathering, they practically populated the whole world. They reached Europe, Asia and America, etc. And then, when this glaciation that abounds with water, flora and fauna ends, they become sedentary and the agricultural society begins.

That agricultural society was great, it lasted for 10 thousand years, it was great in terms of the characters in history, the most important characters in history lived there, from religious history to scientific, artistic, musical, political, the philosophical, all the great characters lived during those 10 thousand years. From Abraham, Moses, Christ, Muhammad, Newton, Beethoven, Leonardo Da Vinci, Socrates, Plato, all the great characters lived in that society.

However, that society had certain paradigms that were based mainly on the exploitation of man by man.

They settled down and began to look for how to conquer their neighbor, how to make war with him, plunder, become slaves, etc. And during those 10,000 years they lived and grew despite great advances in all branches of human life, including construction, the great cathedrals, bridges, arch, vault, etc. Despite that, man was exploited by man. Slavery was usual throughout the world, human rights did not exist, care for the environment, social immobility, etc.

And there is a brutal change in civilization, which is the third stage in which humanity has lived, which is industrial society, it appears with the steam engine, then with the internal combustion engine and then with the electricity engine, and there is a total change of paradigms.

Why am I saying this?

I point this out because the change from agricultural society to the change of industrial society was a great change due to the paradigm shift, which caused great problems, great wars and many conflicts despite the fact that the 13 founding fathers of the United States had established in his letter of independence, liberty, still followed slavery, from the American civil war to the fight of the industrial north against the agricultural and slave south; the French revolution; the Russian revolution; Mexican Revolution; the religious transformation that went from monolithic monarchies to societies that were dictatorships; the first war; the second war. They are the struggle for changes in agricultural society and industrial society.

There, the country that managed to anticipate extraordinarily everything is the United States, since it was born with the concept of freedom, democracy and precepts that are still valid today and we are looking for them that continue to transform the world. This industrial revolution allowed the countries that were pioneers in this sense to advance in development. All of these changes were made in the nineteenth century.

We did them in Mexico in the twentieth century mainly because of the great economic depression in the United States after the Mexican Revolution, Mexico having to find solutions within the country. And he launched a very interesting campaign called "the nationalist campaign, consume what the country produces" that, without being exclusive of foreign investment and foreign trade, placed great emphasis on national growth, on the transformation of the agricultural, rural and self-consumption society to an urban and industrial society. That allowed Mexico at that time to be called "the Mexican miracle" to grow 6.17 percent annually for 50 years.

Mexico grew consistently despite having good and bad governments, little or a lot of inflation, wars, etc. This nationalist campaign begins in a revolutionary block of Congress and the chambers of commerce in a relationship between government and private initiative. One of his strategies was to keep the exchange rate undervalued to import less and export more and give spaces for the private sector to develop. That was a great urban conversion too.

It was when Mexico City and all the cities began to expand in a remarkable way. Thus grew 50 years that way. It culminates or has its brightest moment, I would say, when for twelve years with Secretary Alberto Ortiz Mena Mexico grows to 6.8% with inflation of just over 2%, an inflation even less than that of the United States. We also grew comprehensively seeking the development of the financial, industrial, and agricultural sectors. At that time, tourism was one of the most important factors of foreign currency income in the country.

Despite the wise left, the extreme left within the constitution, of the problem with the OAS in which Mexico stayed with relations with Cuba, from 1968, despite all those problems we grew to 6.8. And then come some changes that end up creating the great problem of foreign debt in '82 that we all know.

Unfortunately, since that time we have been growing at just over 2 % and the truth is that it has helped us a lot as an escape valve to give employment to the fact that so many Mexicans have gone to the United States 400 or 500 thousand sometimes, a year. And the remittances that we all know are substantial. They have helped their families, but in the end, we have not been able to retain those people who are leaving who are the best, the most hard-working, those who are taking risks, those who decide to seek a better future. During this period, we have missed several opportunities.

I would say that one of them and that we all knew was the oil "boom" of the late 70s and early 80s when oil rose from $ 3, with OPEC also up to $ 40. And that we became oil producers and exporters but that we did not take advantage of those revenues that were in the order of 50 billion dollars. Not only do we spend them, but we also get into debt in a similar amount. That crisis came. A few years later, the flow of external savings that occurs substantially in 1991 to 1994, when there is a lot of money coming in, we did not take advantage of it, instead of making productive investment, we lost a lot in current spending.

In all cases we have passed that.

In 2000 it also happened to us, that oil rose again and the oil revenues of those last years are in the order of 800 billion dollars, which is a lot of money. And well, I would also like to stress that the Free Trade Agreement has also given us large inflows of income, we have had significant trade surplus revenues with the United States, but, I think we have also wasted those flows to invest productively in Mexico and that the contents of that export were substantially national.

There are some industries where we have it, in the automotive industry, for example, but it would seem that a good part of the supplies of these products were consumed in Mexico because despite that 60,000 surplus that we have with the United States, we end up running deficits with most countries, perhaps excepting some in Central America. But I think there is a great opportunity field for many of those products that we import to be made here. In other words, a kind of modern import substitution, but no longer under protections as it was in the 60s and 70s of the industrial sectors, but rather, seeking to have these changes efficiently and competitively.

Well, we are on the subject of this meeting "What are the options for the future of Mexico." I dare to affirm, to insist, to return and comment that I still think that the options are the ones we made in 2005 in the Chapultepec agreement. It is called that because it was signed at the Chapultepec Castle, on that occasion civil society represented by academics, intellectuals, labor unions, including opposites, the labor and independent congress, the peasants, the teachers union, the media, businessmen, we all signed that agreement and it was subsequently signed at CONAGO, the presidential candidates also signed it and I think it is still in force. And yes, I am going to allow myself to mention what the points are. Because to be able to solve it and look for the best options, there is no doubt that it is necessary to have clear, precise objectives and instruments, to be able to have a defined course and that this can become state policies so that they do not depend on a government, but they are policies that are continued regardless of the government in charge because there are many projects that are long-term.

In these five points in which we summarize the national objectives that we present and are part of that agreement, we have five central objectives.

The first is the rule of law and public security. Consolidate a State of law in a democratic regime that guarantees freedoms, human and social rights, and physical and legal security.

The second is development with justice, economic growth and employment. Not only the numerical part of economic growth but with a link to the important social aspect, and there is no doubt that employment is the most important or only factor in the fight against poverty and that allows growth to be fed back, that means bringing people who are still marginalized in self-consumption to incorporate it into the modern economy, training, education, greater opportunity and better employment options and to strengthen the market.

The third is to form and develop human and social capital. This means more and better universal health and more and better universal education and of course culture.

The fourth is the development of physical capital. Accelerate the construction of infrastructure and housing plans.

The fifth is to make public administration reforms to make it more effective, transparent and at the service of citizens." (Slim, 2017)

CHER WANG
Co-founder and chairperson of HTC Corporation

Live your reality.

"Good afternoon ladies and gentlemen it´s good to see so many friends and partners here today. I'm very fond of Barcelona. I spent quite a long time here in Barcelona early in my career showing our PC malleable performance to customers all over Europe. Back then not too many people had a personal computer, within a few years most of people has one. While I was dragging my 25 kilo computers up and down a trend across Europe who I exhausted I saw the dream about a small computer that fits into my hand that I could use to call my friends or listen to music; as soon as Windows came out I started HTC with my partners to achieve that dream.

We have introduced some of the most advanced a beautiful smartphones thing including the world's first enjoy phone and the first fortune phone which won so many bests in show awards at Mobile Congress. It´s remarkable to think then no one had a smartphone, now everyone has one and we can't live without them. They always use it 24 hours a day all that to your heart, our main connection to our friends and family.

Mobile Congress was also the stage for the global launch of HTC Vive three years ago, who we introduced the world's first room scale VR. Recently we have also added to revive family a standalone VR in China by Focus. And the world's most premium VR Vive pro. We're in over 200 awards globally, Vive is the start of an exciting journey into the future. Vive has a vision, the convergence of technology with humanity where unleash human imagination.

When we step into virtual reality there's a whole new world of experiences that will change our lives. Where virtual reality was been around for 50 years it's a debunks built in computing power mobility and the interactive technology; that's delivering the promise of VR and making it accessible for the first time. HTC Vive has been at the forefront of creating the premium VR experience raising the bar for content developers to imagine bigger and better. That's why there are over 3000 content titles today with many more on horizon as people realize the potential of this technology.

With VR we can push boundary with our creativity, we can travel to all corners of the earth and beyond; we can do the impossible, we can convey our feelings to our loved ones exactly as we intended. Total immersion creates a powerful sense of empathy, we can truly put ourselves in the shoes of a refugee, an astronaut, or an Olympic skier racing down the slope, we can experience that other experience whether rich or poor, able-bodied or handicapped. As a Chinese philosopher XunZi said: "Seeing is better than hearing, but experiencing is everything." To give you an idea USA today recently posted a video of a disabled man who when virtually skiing with the HTC Vive. It's just deeply moving to see how I've allowed him to feel free again. And this is why I believe that Vive is the great equalizer anyone can enjoy the same experience. It is truly by the people, for the people and share with the people.

Today we are creating by reality the convergence of VR AR 5g and AI where humans interact with virtual and augmented reality environments naturally. Now we are at MWC as the 5G. Our lives have become so dependent on the internet and connectivity we can barely imagine live without it. 5G is becoming and the wizard will come a whole new era of experiences that will truly revolutionize the way we live, work and play, Species or tens of gigabits per second will be transformational, we'll be able to experience and share great quality content anywhere in real time. 5G is a perfect matching technology for VR and AR to real time each computing and life speed data transmission, 5G were massively enlarged VR and AR compatibilities by leveraging super computing power in the cloud where lowering device power consumption.

VR and AR will no longer be constrained to local hardware in storage. Virtual and Augmented reality apart of the virtually continuum there will be combined in different proportions in devices in the future depending on our needs. Car computing over 5G were enable every single VR and AR terminal to be the most power device in the world bringing a more immersive experience than ever. Smartphone will continue to play a vital part in the ecosystem and there will be the first step to 5G for most of us. Smartphones may look different from the shiny rectangles that we know and love today. I think they will also take on all of forms at 5G reduces a need for device-based computing power. In the future the screen may be decoupled away for smartphone and displayed to our VR AR these devices, or even project unto our eyes.

5G will enable the true potential of internet of things with a trillion sensors on a hundred billion connected devices making things work better. Actually, we're getting retailer from all over the world and the bring to us in no time. This brings me to another essential component of Vive Reality Artificial Intelligence; recent advances in artificial intelligence and machine learning take advantage of increasing data and processing power. Today we spend significant time understand how get your work, in the future our cages will know us in many cases better than we know ourselves. AI will truly understand what we need. VR and AR will be the most essential portal to assess the power of AI.

AI will the intelligence to all machine devices and people just like electricity gives us power. I believe that we will add AI through the network to almost everything. AI will be a woven into our everyday life. Learning is so important for us and lifelong learning is becoming vital, with the AI will be able to personalize lessons by seeking the true needs for each person. A world needs from each person, a world it will help us assess all required resources instantly and finish tasks more efficiently for healthcare its applications are almost boundless improving diagnosis, training doctors, recommended treatments, health planes, and so much more. Using VR and AR as a portal together with AI we can use all senses and body to experience, learn, and recall. A partner of ours has a technology for sticking together MRI scan to create a 3d environment for human organs. Helping bankers plan, and perform critical surgeries better than ever possible before.

What I find so beautiful is how it helps patients understand their illness and make it less scary. A friend of mine, a neurosurgeon told me about a little girl who had a large cheeky tumor in her brain, she hadn't smoked for a long time and a strain on her parents was enormous. Two days before the operation my doctor friend put an HTC Vive on the little girl, and was transported into her brain. And she walks around her brain, that doctor pointed out the tumor and told her he will remove the tumor from her, when she saw the tumor she reached out for and she tried to grab an editorial way with a big smile on her. Her parents standing beside her gave a big sigh of relief all the Atenas from week, so, sleepless night washed away. I delighted to say the surgery was successful and the little girl is happily back at the school. It is so important that we harness the power of these disruptive technologies and use it for good. As it says in the Bible: "from the one who has been entrusted with much, much more will be asked." That's why we created VR for impact lives. It's a 10 million dollars initiatives to inspire innovators awareness around the United Nations sustainable development goals.

Experiences that can make us more proactive in helping humanity solve some of the most difficult challenges facing our world today. Imagine you become a big beautiful tree in the rain forest and we are cut off and burned, we can better view the pain of 50,000 acres of rainforest disappearing every single day, a major factor for global warming. It is only when we take the best of what makes us as human and combined with the latest in technology that we can unleash our imagination and passion and make our dreams come true. Looking back in my personal journey to get here today, from PC motherboards to smartphones; to virtual reality all of our innovations were created with the purpose to benefit the humankind.

Friend and partners let's work together as an industry and as a society we definitely will create a better world for us and for our future generations. Please join us on this important journey to Vive Reality. Thank you very much. Have a pressure." (Wang, 2018)

FREDERICK W. SMITH
Founder, CEO and President of FedEx

How far do you want to look?

"This is an untold story about FedEx, because when we started, virtually nothing that we do today was permissible under the laws that existed at the time. For starters, the first thing we were involved in was to change the regulations that permitted you to fly small airplanes without economic regulations by the Federal Government. Then, after that we were heavily involved in the deregulation of air cargo in 1977. The deregulation of surface transportation by the Federal Government in 1980. And then finally, all through the decades of the 90s and the first part of this century we were involved in liberalizing the heavily regulated global airline industry. And absent all of those things we could have never done what we did and had profound effects on the economy of the world in the United States. I'll give you one statistic here that's very important. Logistics cost was a percentage of GDP about 14 and maybe 14.5% before all this starting. Now, they are less than 9%. Huge productivity improvements, great wealth improvements. In China today, for example, they are 20%.

[…] It was absolutely a key and I think it in part came from my service in the Marine Corps which emphasizes leadership principles. But much more importantly it was the recognition that in a high-performance service organization is not the people at the top, that are the most important folks in the equation it is the customer service people. So, you almost have to think of an inverted pyramid. So, the front-line teammates are the ones that need to be highly motivated to deliver that impeccable service. So, people service profit is as important to the success of FedEx as any other thing that we did in the early days.

[…] We realized relatively early that we had to be as close to perfect in the delivering of our services as humanly possible. It became quickly apparent to everyone that with the importance of the type of commerce we were carrying these critical items, we had to keep up with every one of them in a custodial fashion. So, that led us to developing the package tracking system that today has taken were granted by everyone. But in those days, it didn't exist and it required us to create a whole new set of technologies to be able to keep up with each and every item discretely, just as if we were putting it under our arms and carrying it individually. It was that recognition that led us into this type of extreme focus on information technology and we had outstanding 'Chief Information Officers' from the very start of the company.

[...] Similar to the information technology focus, we also recognized relatively early that there was an enormous revolution underway management. After World War II the Japanese actually picked up the quality management techniques that had been developed by the United States Defense industries, so we adopted those quality management methodologies for the simple reason that our customers demanded impeccable quality. and the methods showed that the improvement in quality not only increases customer satisfaction and prevents the lost customers, but it reduces costs [...] and the QDM system that we have today which is in every corner of FedEx is essential to the management of the company. Because again just as predicted, quality is free because it makes the customers happy and it lowers the costs and it makes people ability to do their work easier.

[...] I think my service in the Marine Corps was one of the most important things that happened to me in my life and it was very profound, as it relates to FedEx because the Marine Corps and for that matter, the US Military in general is the greatest teacher of leadership principles in the world. And, in fact, our management school not by accident it's called the Leadership Institute because the first and most important thing that we have to establish in every one of our first-line and second-line managers is that they can be effective leaders in the service industries like we are in. It requires you to withdraw that discretionary effort every day to achieve as we now call it the Purple Promise; I will make every FedEx experience outstanding.

[...] I think FedEx would have been an overnight success except for the first Arab oil embargo in 1973. [...] And we participated in this Energy Security Leadership Council which has been very effective in Washington in trying to maximize US oil and gas production, while at the same time conserving as much as possible through fuel efficiency standards and alternate technologies. And it all stems from that early experience in 1973 where we were almost killed in the cradle [...] a little-known story is there were actually two start dates. The start date in

March was so abysmal that we stopped it and put it off and read April regrouped. And I think maybe it would have taken a relatively large table to sort them, but they could have been sorted on a one table. I think there's 180 somebody shipments.

[...] I think the prospects for FedEx are phenomenal. I am very proud of the things we have accomplished in the past; I am deeply grateful to all of the tens of thousands of men and women who built FedEx it has truly been a team effort, but as I am fond of saying: you aren't seen nothing yet. The size and scope of FedEx today is almost impossible to duplicate, and as a consequence the economic growth that will come in the years ahead will propel FedEx to even bigger heights and greater opportunities for our teammates and owner share owners. So, I am very optimistic about the future. We have got all of the pieces in place to be a very successful company as far into the future as one wants to look. So, my only regret is at age 69 I won't see or coming up to 69, I won't be there to see the next forty years, I do not presume, but it´s going to be exciting." (Smith, 2013)

Pouring the Orange juice on business
Marketing

Who should ultimately design the product? The customer, of course
PHILIP KOTLER
American marketing author, consultant, and professor

As the second ingredient of the cocktail, their participation is to develop content that generates memory in your business. Its primary objective is to harmonize the active substance will enliven malleability of the brand in the market, with the aim of share the qualities of your business and the demands of your target market.

To get to know the word marketing is necessary to look at its origins.

According to Etimonline.com dictionary (2014) the *market* word comes from Latin *mercatus*, which means buying and selling, trading, market. Which served as the source for many languages including: *mercato* in Italian, *mercado* in Spanish, *markt* in German, for example. In Anglo Norman *marchiet* from Old French; were using to mean a meeting at a fixed time for buying and selling livestock and provisions in the old French market of northern; subsequently used as *marché* in modern French, and as *market* in the English, market or sell and trade, *marketing*.

According to Castillo & Bond (1987) the term *marketing* comes from the word *market* and the *ing* completion means effect an action.

In the sixties the Language Academy of Colombia proposed for adoption by *La Real Academia Española (RAE)* [The Royal Spanish Academy] (2012), which defines it as "a set of principles and practices that seek increased trade, especially increased demand."

Santesmases, Sanchez, & Valderrey (2003) mention that the term *marketing* has been consolidated in Spain and in some Spanish-speaking countries, so that the word *marketing* has a wide international recognition both academia and professionally. They add that although Mexico uses the translating *mercadotecnia*, today *marketing* has a widespread use, and not only applies to the company in exchange for economic, goods or services, but also in activities that are not for profit even ideas.

Marketing is a young discipline, with a very recent scientific development, characterized by multiple attempts to define and determine its nature and scope, which has resulted in numerous academic disputes, business and society, although marketing it is something that every day we hear more and applies to a greater extent, ignorance of what really is this discipline is still very significant.

So marketing is considered from different points of view:

1.   An academic discipline under study and research at the university.

2.   A professional discipline, application in business and other institutions that serve a market in particular and society in general.

3.   A philosophy because it is an attitude or way of thinking about the exchange relationship between a company that offers its products to market.

4.   A technique such as specific mode of carrying out the exchange relationship of identifying the gap, create and develop the object approach, to serve demand.

Butler (mentioned by Taylor & Shaw, 1990) defines it as how to put a product on the market considering and resolving many problems that go beyond considering selling, personnel takes just and advertising.

Santesmases et al. (2003) emphasizes that marketing has been used in various fields of study that has been given focus in different areas:

1.   Social Marketing: It serves the cause of non-governmental organizations with tools to make further donations and contributions, communicating their goals and results to the target audience, show through their management and invites people to collaborate.

2.   Noncommercial Marketing: Modifies behavior or attitudes of a segment of the population adapts to the mission and goals of a non-trading company to improve their situation, encouraging or discouraging social or cause social ideas.

3.   Marketing utility: Get closer between government service providers and their customers or citizens, according to the performance of official institutions that directly impact on improving the quality of life of the population.

4. Political marketing: Cultivate the attention, interest and preference of the target market through a person's artistic, sporting and political arena when it also puts in the market for votes in order to maximize your preference.

5. Commercial Marketing: defines Fisher (1988) "is one that sells goods and / or services in an effort to gain economic profit."

According to Taylor & Shaw (1990) in most companies the marketing function is not fully developed due to various reasons:

1. Recent origins of marketing: marketing is a relatively new commercial discipline and often confused with two of its sub-functions such as sales or advertising.

2. Hostility towards marketing: strong vested interest in the company refuse to accept marketing and this must fight an uphill battle to establish their role, scope and authority.

3. Law of slow learning: marketing goes through several stages of misunderstanding, as it grows in the company.

4. Law quickly forgotten: marketing principles tend to be forgotten with the success and need to remember to executives with some regularity.

Santesmases, et al., (2003) allude to that marketing is a mindset, a philosophy of direction on how to understand the terms of trade of products and services of an organization with the market.

Basic Concept: The marketing process analyzes the selection of target market and product opportunities to develop the design with the marketing mix to achieve a successful business project.

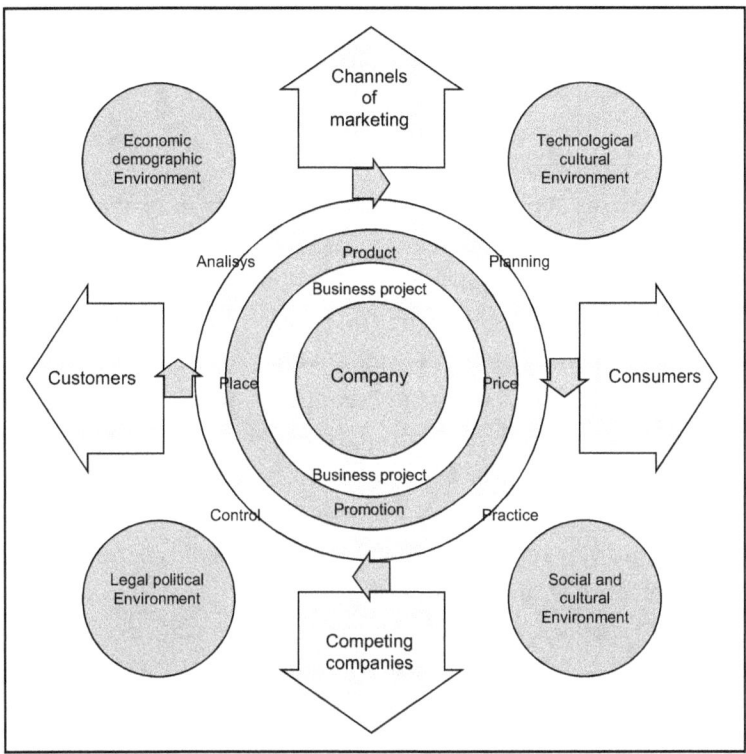

The marketing process and the factors influencing strategy of the company. Adapted from: Kotler, Philip; Amstrong, Gary. *Fundamentos de marketing*. [Principles of marketing] Mexico: Pearson Education, 2003. 589 pp. p. 49.

Marketing and consumer

Offer a customized product or service is one of the most effective ways to increase customer engagement

DON PEPPERS

American business executive, author and keynote speaker

To Santesmases et al., (2003) the trading activity or exchange of goods and services is one of the first who carried out the human being as he was associated with others of their species.

Taylor & Shaw (1990) argue that marketing goes back to the emergence of humanity and is considered one of the oldest professions in the world, this activity, with the passage of time and the increasing number and complexity of trade, has evolved much in the way of understanding and practice.

Stresses that marketing has evolved from its early origins in the distribution and sale into a whole philosophy aimed dynamically connect to any organization with its markets:

• 6000 years ago, the field of marketing is constituted. This is noted when humanity celebrates its first exchange, namely when two parties surplus resorted to barter as an alternative to own property.

• Barter evolved to the sale, which received high expression in very primitive civilizations.

• In the year of 1650, Japan's first member of the Mitzui family, is set in Tokyo as a trader and opened the first department store, anticipating 250 years to the policies of Sears by acting as a buyer for its customers, design products suitable for them and create sources for its production, the principle "is your money back no questions asked" and the idea of offering a variety of products to its customers.

• Around 1850 Cyrus H. McCormick clearly sees marketing as unique and central role of business enterprise, creating a customer as a particular task of management and gave the basics of modern marketing: market research and analysis, the concept of market position, pricing policies, vendor and customer service, spare parts supply and credit for the payment of subscriptions.

- In the early twentieth century marketing was first used in the United States but with a different meaning today. In those dates began to be taught in American universities courses on this new discipline and soon after, the first books were published.

- In the early 1900s the term "marketing" first appeared in collegiate titles.

- In 1905 W. E. Kreusi teaches a course at the University of Pennsylvania under the name of "Product Marketing."

- In 1910 Ralph Stan Butler offered a course entitled "Marketing Methods" at the University of Wisconsin.

- In 1911, the United States, the Curtis Publishing Company, installs the first marketing research department called "Commercial research."

- Santesmases et al., (2003) highlights that marketing began to penetrate the consciousness of different industries at different times. A few companies like General Electric, General Motors, Sears and Procter & Gamble, were among the first to realize their potential; this spread rapidly to companies of industrial products and consumer packaged goods.

- Coca Carasila (2008) says that in 1922 began to use radio signals as an advertising medium, and the first commercial arise in this area, which had an abysmal growth in just a decade.

- Were the universities that began to study the market and the influence of brands in people, but the global economic crisis in 1929 that followed during the decade of the 30, had devastating effects on rich and poor societies, people ran out employment, factories stopped production and marketing of products was relegated.

- In 1934 makes its appearance the American Marketing Journal, which from 1936 became the Journal of Marketing, and in 1937 the "American Marketing Association" (AMA) is created to promote the scientific study of marketing.

- The radio was the preferred mass media for advertising campaigns, until 1941 when advertising comes on TV.

- In 1945 comes the concern for the scientific content of marketing, as an example Converse (cited by Coca, 2008) in that year he published the article "The development of the Science of Marketing" in the Journal of Marketing, which can be considered as the beginning of the debate on the science of marketing.

• Early as 1950 Theodore Levitt introduces concepts such as target market and market segmentation, with the premise that advertising and sales efforts should be directed to the public that will be a potential customer for products, so begins the massive use of media communication for advertising purposes. The rise of television flourishes while the radio down, so do new strategies like telemarketing due to the large growth of households with telephone.

• From the 60s such limits are extended as in 1965, Ohio University defines marketing as the process by which a company anticipates, postponed or satisfies the demand structure of economic goods and services, through the conception, promotion, exchange and physical distribution of goods and services.

• Santesmases et al., (2003) notes that in 1969 Philip Kotler and Sydney Levy expanded the concept to include the marketing of non-profit institutions and public marketing, with products and customers, and perform activities such as those made in companies.

• In 1971 Philip Kotler and Gerald Zaltman, included social marketing aimed at influencing the acceptance of social ideas. In any case, it is the exchanges of (economic or otherwise) values benefit the parties to carry it out.

• Coca (2008) mentions that in 1983 according Wind and Robertson, constantly searched the integration between marketing and strategic planning, deriving in some integrative models.

• In 1984 Zeithaml & Zeithaml, declare that the focus of strategic marketing has a strong dose of proactivity with the environment, this vision is imperative conceiving it as a force that the organization can invoke to create change and expand its influence on the environment.

• That same year, Kotler (2009) defines marketing as a social and managerial process by which groups of individuals and organizations get what they want and need, through generating, providing and exchanging products with others.

• Fisher (1988) states that to engage in a social context both as a business, marketing is interested in consumer behavior where it operates not individually but according to environmental influences.

Basic concept: Success in global level business is only assured for those who maintain a solid understanding of its strategic responsibilities, disciplines that underpin and maturity of business diversification. (Adapted from Colmenares, 1992, Intro.)

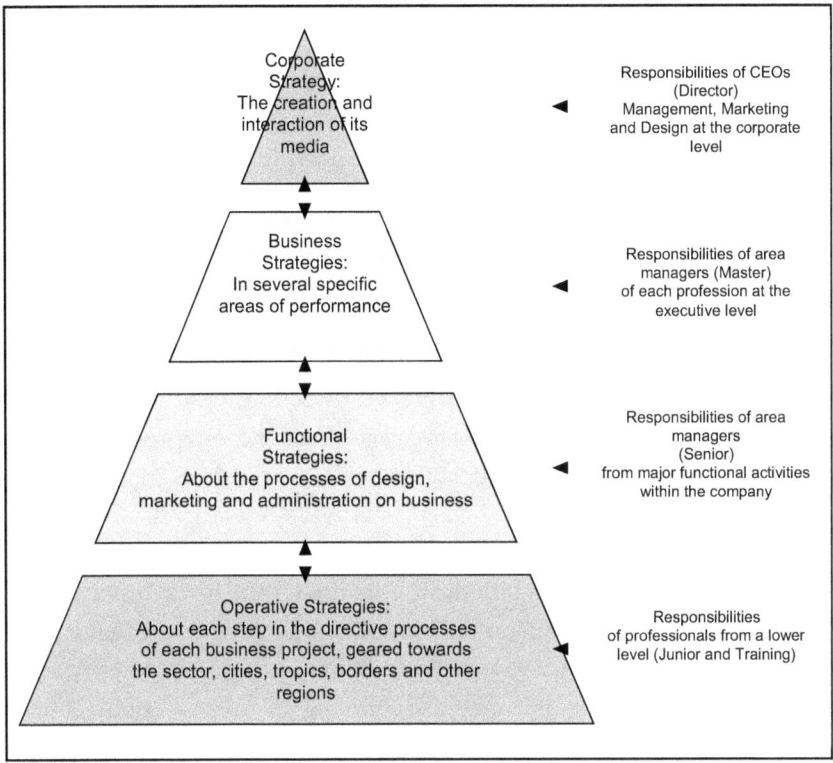

The Pyramid of the creation of the strategy in a company of diversified business. Adapted from: Thompson, Arthur; Strickland, A. J. *Strategic management. Concepts and cases.* USA: Mc Graw Hill, 2004. 398 pp. p. 53.

The aim of marketing

Make the brand experience exceeds the brand perception
STAN RAPP
American executive director of marketing and corporate cofounder

---

According to Schoell and Guiltinan (1991) in a society where free choice practiced when it comes necessary goods, whether products or services, the individual consumer desire becomes strategic. The cumulative force of the wishes of hundreds of millions of consumers in search of a satisfier is the enormous power that activates the marketer development.

Successful marketing is then achieved by selling products that satisfy this desire, anticipating those desires by offering their products; where consumers prefer to buy products that meet their desires in a maximum degree and minimum cost.

The most important characteristics of the current concept of marketing in which includes its position in business can be summarized in providing care to the consumer, however are not many organizations have, in fact, a consumer orientation, although declare that they apply marketing, all they do is, often, advertising or sale, without actually worrying about meeting the needs of potential customers.

So, is that marketing has been classified in various ways:

• Large sectors of society argue that marketing does not seek to meet the real needs of consumers, but creates those needs, and manipulates therefore the consumer is false the statement that "the customer comes first."

• Taylor & Shaw (1990) stress that sometimes marketing managers lose sight of their ultimate goals and focus on short-term gains or dubious benefit to themselves or others. When they lose that sense of higher purpose of marketing, their work becomes unsatisfactory and cynical.

• Schoell and Guiltinan (1991) comment that too, marketing is to organize and direct the use of resources, so that the income from sales of the product or service exceed costs and the surplus is maximized.

- This is, according to Taylor & Shaw (1990) maximizes consumption market whatever the company produces. But he adds that according to this point of view, the marketing manager is a technician who plans sales gains.

The current role of marketing in business does not always have the prominence it deserves.

Frías (2004) notes that erroneously academics and professionals have considered marketing as the art of selling products, but the goal of this discipline is not sales, is to know and understand customers well enough that the product or service generated no only meets the needs, but exceed them where possible, achieving this is sold almost alone.

In the words of Peter Drucker (mentioned by Taylor & Shaw 1990) "Marketing is so basic for business, it cannot be considered separately from a business function is the total enterprise from the perspective of its final outcome, i.e., from the standpoint of customer."

Taylor adds that during the last decades consumer service companies have opened and been input marketing. All large and small, from anywhere in the world, profit or nonprofit are beginning to appreciate the difference between sales and marketing and are organizing to carry out marketing.

In this sense, it is a fact that to effectively fill the effects of marketing in your business and your company, it is first necessary that you are aware of the need of its benefits, consequently assign a department or improve the functions plays and then administering professionally.

Schoell and Guiltinan (1991) comment that in the administration of marketing the masterful challenge is the change due to the growing quickly design innovations in products and services cause a constant pressure to adapt to the competitive market demands.

In this regard, attention should be given to four elements:

1. Establish balance cost with satisfaction: To achieve maximum consumer preference as evenly as possible.

2. Manage the market: In order to form satisfactory volume to the business and the consumer.

3. Understand the nature of the market and part of the mechanical processes involving it towards the product and its effects on the consumer.

4.   Examine the changes occurred in marketing management in the long run to analyze the most important innovations that have been made.

When your company serves these points are involved aspects of marketing that are addressed the customer, giving a strategic sense the objective that both seek to fulfill, which is consummate satisfaction through exchanges of value.

Thus, we can define the strategic marketing in a larger context by analyzing market opportunities powerful and choose best positions following programs and controls created, supporting viable businesses and carrying the purpose and objectives of the company.

Taylor & Shaw (1990) emphasize that within organizations, the marketing department has the major responsibility to initiate the effort to create an attractive play opportunities for the company anywhere within the company from their products or services as well how to create, evaluate and select good ideas that are attractive as opportunities to the business environment:

1.   The internal opportunities of the company: are movements of relevant marketing and these are suggested for the purpose, objectives, growth strategies and portfolio decisions of the company.

It is an attractive event relevant marketing action in which particular companies probably enjoy a differential advantage. Every company has distinctive competencies, namely things you can do especially well.

2.   The environmental opportunities: are market possibilities of a company, while there are unmet needs.

In different industries there are great opportunities to create new and better methods for market but not necessarily represent an opportunity for some specific company. All environmental opportunity has specific requirements of success.

It is for this reason that the main technical contribution of strategic marketing is to evaluate the sales potential of each opportunity with useful methods to achieve serve the market.

By regard to Frías (2004) states that the objective of marketing in business fulfills the function of plan and create products and services enabling obtain a higher standard of living.

Basic concept: In the process of marketing, the development of a new product requires an accurate communication to be useful, that excites the consumer and generates a higher standard of living.

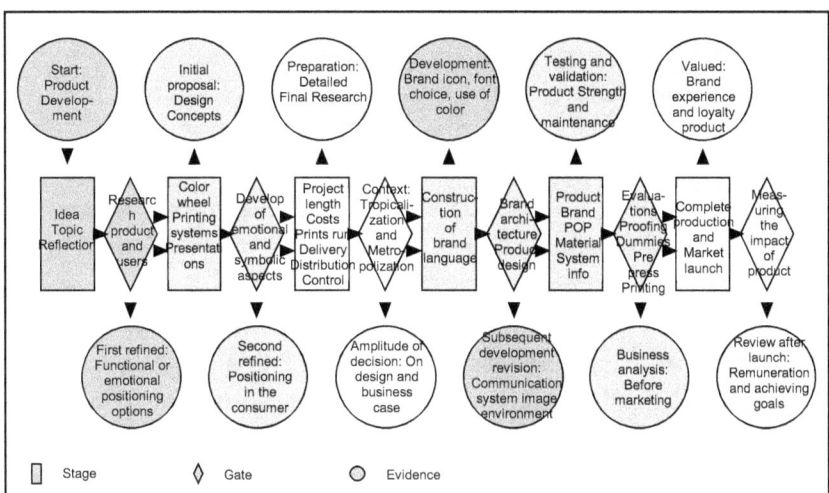

Gate stage system in developing a new product to market. Adapted from: Mullins, J.; Boyd, H.; Walker O.; Larreché, JC. *Administración de marketing. Un enfoque en la toma estratégica de decisiones.* [Marketing Management: A Strategic Decision-Making Approach] Mexico: Mc Graw Hill Interamericana, 2007, 519 pp. p. 258. And: Mono diseño; Charlotte Rivers; Clare Dowdy. *Identidad corporativa: del brief a la solución final. [Branding: From Brief to Finished Solution]* Barcelona: GG. Diseño, 2006, 158 pp. pp. 1&158.

The management of strategic marketing

*If you think good design is expensive, you should look at the costs
of bad design*
RALF SPETH
Important engineer and executive automotive German

For Lamb, Hair, & McDaniel (2011) marketing management is understood as designing activities related to the objectives and changes in the market environment.

Santesmases et al., (2003) propose that a director who plans marketing must make marketing decisions based on their judgment of the consumer response to cost-satisfaction aspects of products designed and supplying a company as well as in assessing its ability to educate that consumer response.

Munch (2009) notes that in large corporations, decision making effecting marketing managers are in charge of professional executives dedicated exclusively to the area where they also have specialists in their field. And in SMEs is rare to find companies with widely developed marketing departments.

The importance of the marketing department in a company focuses on gathering facts and factors influencing the market, to create what the consumer wants, desires and needs, distributing it so that it is available at the right time, in the right place at the most appropriate price.

To Enriquez (2013) the favorable point for the entrepreneur or small business owner is that the development of marketing strategy is not a fantasy that has to be associated with high costs; with the advancement in the electronic communication of content becomes relevant, since the cost generated It is really minimal.

In this sense Contreras (2001) states that the mission is an enduring statement of purpose of a company that distinguishes it from others and scope of operations of a company is in its products and markets.

So your mission statement must indicate the target characteristic that differentiates your company, in a unique way.

Kotler (2009) said that the mission statement is the expression of the purpose of the organization is, what you want to achieve in the wider environment. It also recommends that its construction is oriented towards the market, ie, in terms of meeting the needs of consumers.

Baena (2011) states that it is advisable that the mission statement is made on the market it has to serve, always careful not to fall into marketing myopia, which is to focus the business from a product perspective and not from the market.

In this tenor the most objective remuneration with which you can achieve consumer satisfaction is evaluating their opinion about a product or service requested or acquired for improvement. The marketing tool that manages the sole purpose of satisfying the needs of consumers it is the market study. This determines the factors that influence consumer buying decisions, ergo, analyzes their behavior on their site preferences market.

The American Marketing Association [AMA] (2004) defines market research as "function that links the consumer, customer and public to the seller through -used information to identify and define opportunities and marketing problems; generate, refine and evaluate marketing actions; monitor the performance of marketing; and improve understanding of marketing as a process-. Marketing research specifies the information required to address these issues, designs the method for collecting information, manages and executes the process of data collection, analysis of results, and communicates the findings and their implications."

Fisher (1988) says that when marketing analyzes the market environment, consumer preferences on a market or product are evaluated. According Fisher the market research relates to know who they are or may be consumers or potential customers to identify their characteristics.

Apply it can offer great benefits to your company based on their results, give better data to strengthen the tools of marketing management to increase product demand, the market share and profit.

Such tools are the 4 P's which together are called marketing mix, or product, price, promotion and place.

For the AMA (2014) the marketing mix is controllable variables that the firm uses to pursue the desired sales level in the target market.

Kotler & Amstrong (2003) defined as the 4 P's of the marketing mix:

1. Product: The combination of goods and services that the company offers to the target market. Product design.

2. Price: The amount of money that customers have to pay for the product. The product price.

3. Promotion: Involves activities that communicate the benefits of the product and persuade target customers to buy it. The promotion that brings the product to the consumer.

4. Place: Also known as distribution includes the activities of the company that makes the product will be available to target consumers. The place to exhibit and put in the hands of the consumer to the product.

These four elements are the basic tools of marketing director, which must base their decisions so that by combining offer benefits to the company.

The 4 variables are understood more clearly form when applied in market research:

1. Knowing whether the consumer meets your needs or desires with the acquisition of the *product*.

2. Knowing if the consumer is satisfied with the *price* or considers money to pay is greater than the benefit obtained.

3. Knowing the details of the means of *promotion* in greater impact or influence it has had on the consumer.

4. Knowing lastly if the consumer buys your product in the distribution site or *place* at the right time.

Against the background described each P will create its strategy:

1. For the product: its value added, scilicet, render our products in a higher than our competitor idea.

2. For the price, that can be modified, from being diminished by the low-cost production to offer attractive discounts to return the product purchase.

3. To promote: the media or ideas expressed our message to the consumer, the more concrete and attractive the more favorable communication will result.

4. For the place: choosing the right place to carry out the distribution, a relationship between the company expanded its market to bring the product to the customer.

It is important to remember that the implementation of the marketing mix should be based on market research, taking into account competition and trends, to provide the bases and tools needed on the profitability of the strategy is generated.

Faced with the responsibility of the strategy work, every marketing effort should be linked to what is meant by Lamb, Hair, & McDaniel (2011) argue that introducing situational analysis better known as SWOT, identification of internal and external environment is determined in which the sale of the product or service is performed.

Basic Concept: The proper conformation of the strategy begins with the identification of opportunities and risks in the external environment to put into action opportunities with company resources to implement the strategy.

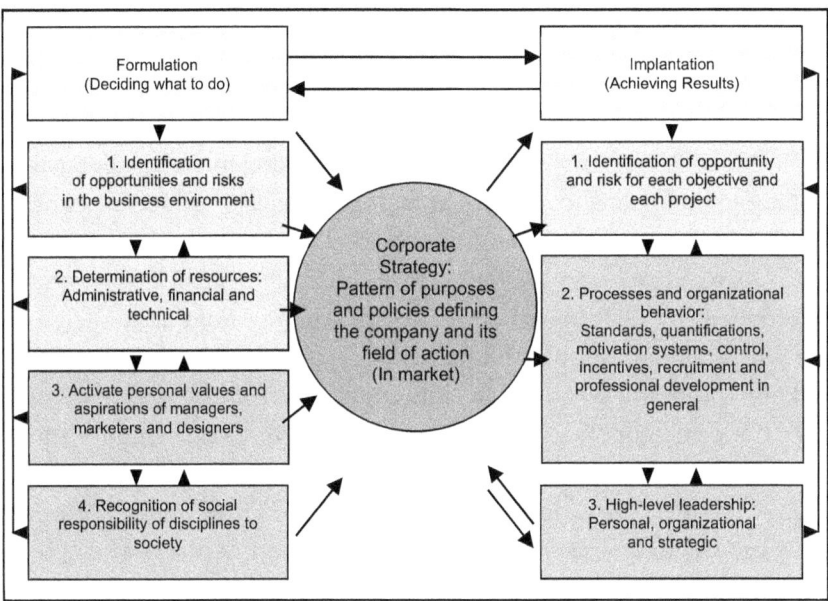

The implementation of the strategy in a company. Adapted from: Mintzberg, Henry; J. Brian; J. Voyer. *El proceso estratégico. Conceptos, contextos y casos.* [The strategic process. Concepts, contexts and cases]. Mexico: Prentice Hall Hispanoamericana, 1997. 641 pp. p. 54.

The marketing planning

You have to live with your product. You must imbibe it. You have to saturate of it. You must get to the heart of it. Yes, but if there is not an original concept that can be communicated to the reader, you cannot be creative
WILLIAM BERNBACH
American advertising creative director

In a business environment where debated by the market both retail and wholesale large scale, gain an advantage that allows them to compete better is the crucial basis for strategic marketing why, is based on planning. The marketing department uses the marketing plan as an essential tool for operation.

Enriquez (2013) says that a large corporation or a small business looking to compete successfully in marketing their products or services, should plan and establish four initial marketing tactics:

1.   Create an unmistakable brand identity: Business success is determined by its powerful ability to communicate accurately and provide a defined, simple and consistent experience. In short it is called making "branding," and when done right, it ensures a business in the minds of customers that the company needs. The brand identity should be strong, clear, and created before any other action marketing.

2.   Identify the target audience to connect with him: What the company has to offer, someone specific wants and needs. And this is not everyone. The target is only those people who need it, and exactly, those who are willing to pay for it. Identify well the specific group of consumers having characteristics in times, places and special circumstances, will unveil a connection to attract them.

3.   Generate compelling offers to attract customers like a magnet: It is working on providing customers what excites them and want to feel, to arrive visualize how these services can meet these feelings. The customer wants to know "What's that to me?" Enter the feeling and create offers that excite their customers. Make them their delirious fans. All buying decisions are based on emotion and feeling.

4.   Land achievable marketing plan: Do everything required for the product or service becomes available, more convenient and more

profitable. The marketing plan should set the overview to provide a comprehensive approach basing on the client. Developing a plan automatically achieve an advantage over most of the competition, provided that this is objective and feasible to achieve business goals.

Properly implement marketing planning can transform any business large or small, in a commercial strength that can extend its scope, with satisfied customers. Its flexibility and dynamism depend largely on the accuracy of the initial work to develop your content.

Sanz de la Tajada, (mentioned in Sainz de Vicuna, 2013) states that the marketing plan is a written document in which a systematic and structured way, anticipated the corresponding analyzes and studies, defining objectives to be achieved in a period of time, as well as programs and means of action to be accurate detailing to achieve the stated objectives within the period expected.

Both (Fischer & Espejo, 2004) and (Stanton, Etzel, & Walker, 2007) suggest that it should draft a document for planning marketing efforts and work throughout the company, this is the strategic marketing plan that develops six major steps:

Stanton et al., (2007) agree:

1.   Situational analysis: Where a SWOT analysis as a diagnostic is included, consumer groups who are directed the company, strategies to satisfy them and the principal measures of performance marketing. It also identifies and evaluates competitors that address the same markets.

2.   Objectives of marketing: They keep a close relationship with corporate goals and strategies. Each objective should receive priority regarding their demands, their results in the area and their preponderance in the organization. Then, resources must be allocated according to these priorities.

3.   Positioning and Differential advantage: The positioning is the result of the preference of the product against competing products in the market and with other products in the same company. The differential advantage will any feature of an organization or brand that consumers perceive desirable and distinct against competition.

4.   Target market and Market demand: Are the target groups of people or organizations to which the company focus its marketing efforts. Then, it includes a forecast of demand, or sales in the target

markets that seem most promising to consider and decide the appropriate segment or alternative.

5.   Mix marketing: is the combination of many aspects of the following four elements: which product is, what its price, how it is promoted and where it distributes. The role of each of these elements is to satisfy the target market and fulfill marketing objectives of the company.

Fischer & Espejo (2004) project also:

6.   Evaluation of results or Control: The tool that will constantly monitor and evaluate each operation of the strategic marketing plan for the end result adheres as closely as possible to the desired.

They add that the advantages of planning favor to:

a)   Encourage the systematic thinking of marketing management.

b)   Improve coordination of all activities of the company.

c)   To guide the organization regarding objectives, policies and strategies that must be carried out.

d)   Avoid that there are surprising developments within the activities of the entire company.

e)   Contribute to have greater participation of executives, to interrelate their responsibilities to changes in company projects and the setting in which it operates.

Taylor & Shaw (1990) say that the main contribution of strategic marketing is to evaluate the sales potential of each opportunity with useful methods to achieve serve the market.

Lamb et al., (2011) point out that the relationship between marketing and strategic planning requires the proper focus of the marketing plan. The decisions that the director of marketing department should do in this plan are inescapable interest of the company.

According to Lamb, decision making is part of the strategic direction, is performed taking into account the benefits that the organization expects in a given period and is based on the matrix product / market, also called Ansoff box. It is a technique for analyzing business that identifies growth opportunities. It may help to consider the implications of business growth through products and markets, traditional or new. Each of these growth options is based on research, influence and internal and external analysis, then work on the strategy chosen.

According to Free-management-ebooks.com (2013) maintains four marketing strategies, the sequence is:

1.   Market penetration: Focusing your sales of existing products or services to your existing markets and achieves growth in market share.

2.   Market development: Focus on developing new markets or market segments for your existing products or services. Promotes demand.

3.   Product Development: Focus on new developments of products or services to your existing markets. Active frequency.

4.   Diversification: Focusing on the development of new products or services for sale in new markets.

To plan the market is necessary market research that you used to collect your representative sample, the necessary data which require converted into the product want to get your target audience.

Basic Concept: The process of planning and executing of a market research has stages that can be understood as a cyclical process, as the research findings presented generate new ideas or new problems amenable to research.

I. DESIGN
1. FORMULATION OF THE PROBLEM: Just posing it properly finds the right answer.
1.1 Discovery: • Discover the existing need to solve. • Value the opportunity. For example, introducing a new product in the range. • Evaluate the strategy adopted by the business address.
1.2. Definition: • Define precise objectives to guide entire process that follows. • It raises the questions or hypotheses that research must solve or contrast. • Answer the question: "Why do we do this research?" • Define an idea of the information needed and how to obtain it.
2. DETERMINATION OF RESEARCH DESIGN: Tackle the problem and its nature.
2.1 Exploratory Design: • Use secondary information sources and qualitative research methods based on small (group dynamics, depth interviews observation, and so on.) samples. • Identify threats and opportunities in the environment. • Define the problems precisely at the level of objectives and questions. • Raises hypotheses explaining the facts to identify basic variables and their possible relationships.
2.2 Conclusively Design: • Contrast the hypotheses formulated after performing an exploratory investigation. • Evaluate and select action alternatives. • Establish relationships between the variables of interest.
2.2.1 Descriptive Design: • Research by surveys, obtaining samples that allow generalizing the results to the population. • Respond to questions: "who," "what," "when," "how much," "how," "where," and "why," quantitatively. • Describe and measure market phenomena that occur frequently. • Determines the degree of association between variables. • Make predictions.
2.2.2 Causal Design: • Estimate how far changes in one variable (controllable independently or treatment) produces changes in other variables (uncontrollable, dependent or effect) in a temporal sequence. • Identify and specify fully the research problem. • Determine which variables or treatments are independent and what the dependent. • Determine the functional relationships between causes and effects. • Its methodology is the experimental method. Controls the external conditions so that one or more variables can be manipulated to test a hypothesis about how it affects another, and all this is usually performed using control groups.
3. PREPARATION: Delimits all previous fieldwork activities.
3.1. Determination of the required information: • Secondary information is that which already exists, is prepared and published. It may have been generated by the company itself or by third parties and can dispose of it because they were stored in the company (internal) itself, or outside (external). The latter can be bibliographical or obtained for free (publications and databases in libraries of public schools), or can be syndicated, or acquired for a price to companies specialized in obtaining information. • The primary information is collected specifically for the research question being addressed because the necessary information has not been previously collected by anyone or you do not have access to it. Therefore, it must be generated through qualitative research (group dynamics, interviews, observation, projective techniques) or quantitative (surveys, experiments, observation).
3.2. Determination of the method of obtaining: • For qualitative techniques such as group dynamics, in-depth interviews, projective techniques or direct observation. These techniques are very flexible; they lack rigid structures and include, typically, a few sample elements (respondents). Allow exploration of the issues and the presentation of hypotheses. • For quantitative techniques: as survey research, direct observation and experiment design. These techniques typically involve the use of structured questionnaires and include a large number of respondents, as they require that the results can be projected to the population. When to confront the research problem is sufficient to obtain secondary information, this subphase will be reduced to the determination of their sources of information, which will take the form of available publications and databases.
3.3. Designing the questionnaire: • The questionnaire is the formal instrument or medium customarily used for collecting reliable and valid primary information. Generally a good questionnaire will be enjoyable and easy to complete. • Gets primary information involves performing a series of special activities such as questionnaire design and the test sample. • Decide assessment scales to be used to measure the variables of interest. So, we will have to choose between comparative or not comparative scales, between scales of a single item or multi-item, ... • Determine the structure (order or sequence of questions) and format (of great importance in self-administered questionnaires). • Make a previous test of it with a small subsample in order to improve before final application.
3.4. Sample design: • The sample is a subset of the population in general representation selected for study. Individuals, households, businesses, ... • Ensures the representativeness of selection, so that the study results can be generalized to the population. • Define the purpose of the study population and identified by a sampling frame. • Determines the method for selecting the elements of the sample from the sampling frame (probability or non-probability) that decisively affects the degree of representativeness of the sample. • Decide on the sample size, aspect that affects the precision of the estimates and the cost of the study. From the set size can be estimated sampling error of the estimates.

TEQUILA SUNRISE FOR BUSINESS

4. FIELD WORK: Collect information with the questionnaire.

4.1. Planning: organization and programming of field work, including preparation of instructions; they must be set the rules concerning how to select interviewees (when and where to select the sample).

4.2. Preparation of interviewers: Includes selection and training. It is intended that interviewers are familiar with a series of general rules and the specific research in which will help. This phase involves the development of a set of instructions on the correct application of the questionnaire and instructions for each of the questions in the questionnaire.

4.3. Conducting interviews: Involves the actual selection of sampling units and conducting the survey. That is, it is the field work itself.

4.4. Control of work: Involves the supervision of surveys conducted by interviewers.

III. ANALYSIS

5. INFORMATION PROCESSING: Give precisely riverbed information obtained.

5.1. Edition: It consists in reviewing the questionnaires received from the field to decide whether they are valid for analysis. The edition involves examining various aspects, some directly on the paper questionnaire and other later (for verification) on the computer support, once the data has been recorded.

The edition leads to the exclusion of those questionnaires that do not meet the minimum quality established by decreasing the size of the sample. Represents a process of controlling the work of interviewers.

The following aspects are discussed mainly:
• No missing pages in the questionnaire.
• That key survey questions have been answered.
• That key survey questions are answered correctly, that is, following the instructions provided.
• That the questionnaire was answered by individuals in the target population.
• That has been completed sample quotas.

In addition, it is also very important to check the following points:
• The consistency in the answers of respondents. For this control questions included in the questionnaire are analyzed. For example, it is not consistent one respondent stating that no known specific brand, but later claims to have ever bought.
• The interviewer does not influence the respondent's answers. To do all questionnaires from the same pollster as a whole are reviewed to determine that no suspicious patterns of response are observed.
• The no falsification of questionnaires by the interviewer. For this makes so-called endorsement, it consists in to call a percentage of respondents to verify that the questionnaire was done actually and effectively.

5.2. Encryption: consists of assigning codes (usually numeric) to each of the response options for each question. This facilitates the recording of data and statistical analysis of the responses from the sample by software. This process usually develops during the design phase of the questionnaire, since it is highly desirable that the codes assigned to each question and answer option appear in the questionnaire to facilitate the process of recording the data to the computer file.

5.3. Designing the database: It consists in make the structure of the file that will contain all the raw data obtained in the field of research. Essentially involves creating variables that represent the concepts measured by the questionnaire. This process also should do it as part of questionnaire design.

5.4. Recording: This involves the transcription of data from paper support (questionnaire) to the computer database prepared. After recording the data, the file contains the coded answers given by all respondents to the questionnaire.

5.5. Verification: This involves a process of editing the recorded data. It is found that the recording contains no errors and that the questionnaires gather maximum quality (coherent answers, no influence of the interviewer, ...).

6. TABULATION AND ANALYSIS: These sub-phases of the entire process.

6.1 Tabulation: The objective is the initial exploration of the obtaining data, providing the basic results. It involves counting and summarizing ordered arrangement of raw data (stored in the file) in a table or other summary format. Equivalent to calculating the frequency distribution of each variable, that is, the count of absolute and relative frequencies each answer choice for each question.

6.2 Analysis: It involves the development of different operations on the raw data, beyond the simple count, in order to get results and conclusions not directly observables, namely not derived from simple observation of the frequency tables. Allow to simplify the information collected with the survey or contained in the data file and draw conclusions about the behavior of the variables. The analysis can be:
• Descriptive: if the objective is to summarize the information from the sample. Descriptive statistics (means, variances, correlations, ...) are used.
• Inference: if the goal is to make judgments about the behavior of the population based on the results of the sample. Inferential statistical techniques (test or hypothesis contrasts) are used.

Furthermore, depending on the number of variables analyzed simultaneously, the analysis can be:
• Univariate: if each variable is studied separately (mean, variance, ...).
• Bivariate: if relations between pairs of variables (correlation, cross tabulation, ...) are analyzed.
• Multivariate: if more than two variables are analyzed simultaneously. Multivariate methods are characterized by their great potential for treatment and simplification of data. The most widely used in market research are the following: correspondence of factorial analysis, principal component analysis, classification analysis (cluster), multidimensional scaling analysis, discriminate analysis, regression analysis, analysis of joint actions (conjoint) analysis of variance and hierarchical segmentation analysis.

Finally, the level of measurement of variables in order to select the most suitable type for data analysis should also be considered. In this sense must differentiate between metric and non-metric data (either ordinal or nominal).

IV. COMMUNICATION OF THE REPORT

7. COMMUNICATION AND PRESENTATION

7.1 Written report and oral presentation: The formal drafting supported in a speech for their projection. As the unique aspects of the study that will know the marketing manager, their assessment will depend largely on the way in which is communicated.
• Include the beginning of the report a short 'summary executive', in a couple of pages summarizes the most relevant from research.
• Start the speech with the target and always be brief, but thorough.
• Include at least the nature of the research problem and research objectives.
• Applied Methodology (consulted sources of information, methods of obtaining information applied, sample selection, analysis techniques used, ...).
• Results obtained.
• Conclusions and recommendations.

Stages of process of market research. Adapted from: EducaMarketing (2005) *Guía para realizar una Investigación de Mercados* [A guide for develop a Market Research] Extremadura, Spain: University of Extremadura.

Competitiveness

The essence of competitiveness is liberated when we make people believe what
they think and do is important and then get out of their way while they do
JACK WELCH
American business executive, author and chemical engineer

To Wikipedia.org (2015), the concept of competitiveness is understood as the ability to generate greater customer satisfaction by offering the association of a lower price compared to some quality; the most competitive companies will take more market share at the expense of less competitive businesses if there are not market failures that prevent it.

The loss of competitiveness describes an increase in production costs, as this will adversely affect the price or profit margin without providing improvements to product quality.

To assimilate the importance of competitiveness and make it work to the business environment need to understand what Porter (1990) considered the basic unit of analysis to understand business competition, is the sector, the business entity where interact a group of competitors who manufacture products or provide services and compete directly with each other.

Porter (1980) said that there, the nature of competition consists of five competitive forces:

1.   The bargaining power of buyers: The powerful clients are able to capture more value if they force down prices, demand better quality or better services which increases costs and generally make participants sector confronted; all this at the expense of industry profitability, especially if they are price sensitive and primarily use their power to press for price reductions.

2.   The bargaining power of suppliers: Powerful providers capture a greater share of value for themselves by charging high prices, restricting the quality or services, or transferring costs to industry participants. When a global corporate raises the prices of additions to a product, contributes to erosion profitability for the other manufacturers of the same product that have very limited possibilities to raise their prices.

3.   The threat of new entrants: New entrants in a sector introduce new capabilities, and a desire to gain market share, putting pressure on prices, costs and the rate of investment needed to compete. They can leverage existing capabilities and cash flows to shake the competition, especially when diversify from other markets. The threat of new entrants, therefore, places limits on the profitability potential of a sector.

4.   The threat of substitute products or services: A substitute performs the same or a similar function as the product of a sector through various forms. The video conferences are a substitute for travel. Plastic is a substitute for aluminum. The e-mail is a substitute for express mail. Also, when a substitute replaces the product of a buyer sector. The sale of turf is threatened when multifamily buildings crowd the suburbs; or when the websites of airlines substitute for travel agents.

5.   The rivalry among existing competitors: This rivalry takes many familiar forms, including price discounts, new products, advertising campaigns and service improvements. A high degree of rivalry limits the profitability of the sector. The degree to which the rivalry reduces profits of an industry depends primarily on the intensity with which companies compete and, secondly, of the basis on which they compete.

Each of these competitive forces reacts according to their intensity within the structure of the sector and this influence companies to choose a position within the same.

Porter adds that the center position is the competitive advantage, which develops two main strategies for competitiveness:

1.   Focus on lower cost or overall cost leadership: It is determined by the ability of a company to design, fabricate or make and to market the products or comparable services more efficiently than its competitors at a low cost.

2.   Focus on differentiation or Differentiation wide: The ability to provide the buyer with a particular product or service superior value with the advantage of being singular in terms of quality, physical characteristics and visual qualities that make it unique and special.

Kotler & Armstrong (2003) allude that have a competitive advantage when competing with companies in the same industry where customer loyalty is won or has any superiority gained by offering consumers greater value than the offered by competitors.

In this sense, Kotler says that the competitive advantage of low costs translates to a reduction in costs as a result of the acquisition of low-cost raw materials, contribution or donation of material for the company or production technology conditions capable of reducing these. The advantage of low cost does not mean that quality is lousy compared to products made with materials more expensive. The intent of this strategy is to sell a product or service at a lower price than the competition.

Lamb et al. (2011) notes that the competitive advantage of differentiation is to add a quality that can be attended by the target market as unique in the market. This attention by the market influences such that the product price moves to a secondary importance. Differentiation can be seen as the inclusion of new applications, technologies or tools to a product.

This advantage should be applied a specific market segmentation serving only a group of people with similar characteristics.

The company must maintain its competitive advantage as long as possible as one of their strategies. Competitive advantage is, "the advantage that the competition cannot copy" and will be renewed when competition achieves copy the differentiating strategy.

Porter (1990) says that to gain a competitive advantage required a set of ideas that are not present in many companies. Most of companies value stability and no change. His constant concern is to protect ideas and old techniques, not create new ones.

In that sense, Mintzberg, et al. (1997) highlights the strategists who want to design their organizations to be efficient using all the resources at their disposal with well-defined parameters. Emphasizes differentiation strategy that relates to offer something that really is different; supported in design, this tries to break with the dominant design, if it exists, and provide unique features.

That is to have emerged new strategies to fortify the competitiveness of enterprises.

Lawrence (1996) express that it is amazing how is that design is still unknown and so misunderstood among entrepreneurs, despite looking for with dire need any potential competitive advantage.

Filson & Lewis (2000) point out that SMEs tend not normally use the design as a significant source of business, which may specifically be due to ignorance of its benefits.

So is that Olson, Slater, & Cooper (2000) assert that exist at the center of any competitive business strategy a set of differentiating competencies that are the resource holding the advantage of the company. A valuable strategy that is increasingly known, but it is still largely ignored as a resource to obtain this advantage is the design.

Basic concept: To manage differentially in the market, will should be recognized to design as an important resource of business and run their specific strategies to the sector in which it competes.

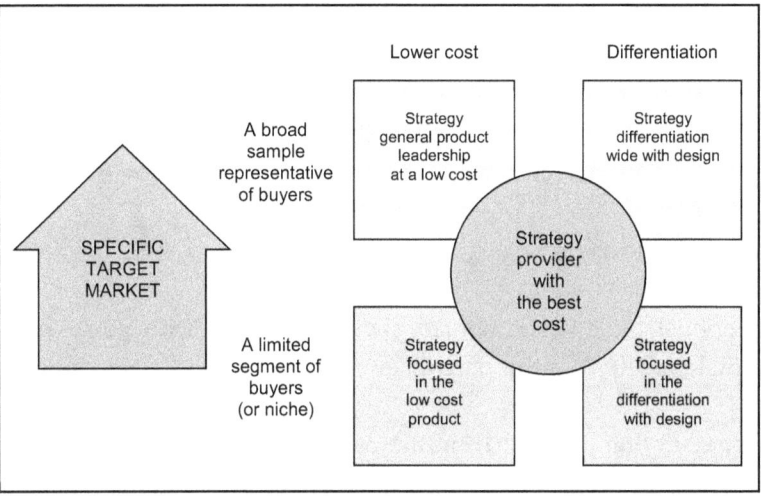

The five generic competitive strategies. Adapted from: Porter, Michael E. *Competitive Strategy*. New York: Free Press, 1980. 407 pp. p. 153.

The ice on background | PART 2
Pervading Orange

There are essentially two things that will make you wise, the books you read and the people you meet
JACK CANFIELD
American author and motivational speaker

MICHAEL DELL
Founder, chairman and CEO of Dell Technologies

Amplify the beginning.

"Seriously, it's an honor to share the stage with some of UT's incredible faculty. To the parents and family members here today: you did it.

Today my family is sharing the celebration. Our daughter Juliette is graduating. Which, as she knows, is something I never quite managed to do. If you don't know, I should confess: I dropped out of UT after two semesters. Let me explain.

As far back as I can remember, I always wanted to go faster. When I was young, I was flipping through a magazine when I saw an ad in the back. By taking one simple test, the ad explained, I could skip high school. Well, I thought that offer was too good to pass up. So, I clipped out the ad and sent away for my high school equivalency exam. My plan was foolproof … except for one problem: I was eight years old.

A few weeks later, our doorbell rang. My mother answered the door. It was a woman from the testing company. "Is Mr. Michael Dell home?"

Right on cue, my mother answered: "Yes, he is … he's taking his bath."

To make a long story short, I graduated from high school — ten years later. Almost as soon as I got to college, I wanted out — and not just because I was living at Dobie. I'd started a business. It was growing exponentially, and at the time, it felt to me like college was a distraction. Real life, I thought, was out there. One point of clarification: when a college freshman says he's dropping out because he's selling something out of his dorm room … it's probably not 10MB hard drives. But that is what I was selling, and it put me on a path that's been more interesting, more challenging, more fulfilling and more fun than I could have ever imagined.

Thirty-five years later, I'm here to tell you that what you've gained here, by completing your degree, will be indispensable "out there." In a world that doesn't wait, you should be proud for taking the time to finish what you started. It took me a lot longer than four years to learn the value of patience. You've also gained the trust and respect of your friends and mentors. Don't take that for granted, because trust and respect are two things that you earn very slowly and can lose all at once … like a 10-win football season. And by the way, you didn't just complete your degree. You completed your University of Texas at Austin degree.

This university is a remarkable place. The scale of its ambition … the diversity of its people and ideas … the emphasis on making a difference … Take it from someone who spent two semesters in Longhorn Nation — and three decades, give or take, in the neighborhood: there's just no place else like it. I appreciate that now in a way that maybe I didn't as a student, when I was in such a hurry.

As a kid, I was fascinated by computing — the idea that we could program a machine to exceed our capabilities. That we could use the power of what's possible to do the impossible. It started when I got my first calculator in elementary school. By junior high, I was staying after school to write programs on my math teacher's Teletype computer terminal. When I finally got my first computer, at age 14, I did what any normal, well-adjusted teenager would do: I took it apart, piece by piece, and examined the circuits. A few years later, I got unbelievably lucky: The National Computer Conference relocated to my hometown of Houston. Thankfully, I had my driver's license — because I couldn't have paid anyone in Houston to take me to the 1982 National Computer Conference.

To understand why, I want you to close your eyes and imagine a state-of-the-art technology conference. The epic stage with space-ship lighting. The photogenic "founders" and "creatives," wearing hoodies and gliding around on scooters.

Now imagine exactly the opposite of that. Imagine a fluorescent-lit room filled with men—and yes, at that time, it was nearly all men—and some of them even wore pocket protectors. To give you a taste of what was on the menu in 1982, the theme of the conference was "Advancing Professionalism." Not, you know, "Changing the World." Advancing. Professionalism. Well, I was in heaven. I probably couldn't have explained why at the time, but I think I know now. What excited me most were the words "personal computer." Now, that, to most of you, probably sounds about as cool as "Advancing Professionalism."

But you have to understand: in 1982, we weren't so far from a time when, if a university had a computer, it was so big they had to build a special building around it. And it took a team of people to operate it. And it had about as much computing power as a vending machine. To go from that to a personal computer… in a word, I knew it would be empowering. I didn't know that computers would become a gigantic industry. I just knew that they were going to help more people do the impossible. When I look back now, it's clear that 1982 was just the beginning. And sooner than you think, you'll look back on 2019 and see: it's still the beginning.

The question is, the beginning of what?

After all, these days, many people are frightened by technology. Rightfully so. Technology is evolving faster than we—and our laws—can keep up. Technology is displacing workers from their jobs, and very possibly, displacing humans as the most intelligent species on Earth. The truth, though, is that I'm a massive optimist. Let me tell you why.

First, even in light of some very serious problems, I find it impossible to overstate technology's potential for good. We know the role technology plays in empowering us—in enabling us to improve our own lives—and we've seen how it empowers others around the world. The democratization of technology over the past few decades has helped to drive a huge increase in human progress. And we're just getting started.

Both my company and our family's foundation are investing in projects that use cutting-edge technologies to solve age-old problems.

We've seen a simple banking app helping families, break out of the cycle of poverty. We've seen massive information networks help girls access education. Tiny satellites are helping us track toxic debris from wildfires. You've probably heard about what's coming down the pike. Self-driving cars. Drone deliveries. But how about some real progress, like the eradication of deafness… and blindness… and paralysis? Neural implants, robotics, and AI will make all these these miracles possible.

When I started Dell 35 years ago, I couldn't have imagined any of this. That's why I made sure people were at the center of everything we did. Not technology. People. In the early days, that meant selling PCs directly to customers. Then came the rise of the internet, smart phones, the cloud and a massive increase in the amount of digital data in the world. To succeed and grow we are constantly learning, transforming, evolving, and staying curious. Just like you will do over the course of your careers. Because this is how progress happens.

That transformation required me to take some of the biggest risks of my life. I wanted to accelerate the pace of our transformation, innovate more aggressively. So, after 25 years as a public company, I decided to take the company private. It was at the time the largest company in the world, by revenues, ever to go private. It worked very well and then we decided to take an even bigger risk—making the largest acquisition in technology history. Everything really is bigger in Texas.

There were plenty of skeptics and back-seat drivers. Actually, I thank them, because for me it was just motivation to prove them all wrong. Now we are public again, stronger than ever, and having our best year ever. More relevant and able to serve more customers than ever before. We are pleased but not satisfied. We're in a race with no finish line and the pace just keeps getting faster. But our goal is not just to make our company grow. Our goal is to enable human progress and potential… and in that regard, we—all of us—have a lot of work to do. I believe we have a responsibility to help ensure that the next generation of even more powerful technology reflects our humanity and our values.

Which brings me to the second reason I'm optimistic about technology:

I have faith in what you're going to do with it. Technology itself is neutral. It's neither good nor bad. Technology can amplify human genius, but it can also amplify human frailty. The choice is ours. The choice is yours. And that is why I'm optimistic. Your generation has already made it clear that you're committed to fairness and justice for all. You are as engaged as any group of graduates who ever walked the 40 acres. You're going to demand that technology not only do new things, but do the right things.

And you see your role in making that so. You have the drive to align your work with a greater purpose. You have the ambition not only to succeed but to serve. This, you might say, is humanity's source code. It's not a coincidence that these values are central at UT. Whatever you majored in, whatever you do after today, living up to that code will not only "Advance Professionalism." It really will change the world. Of course, living up to that code is hard. It's going to demand that you step up... and take risks. Many people never realize what they're capable of because they're afraid to make mistakes. Many people don't stand up for what's right because they're afraid to be wrong. But that's not how changing the world works. Unless you're willing to take risks, you won't have a chance to use your talents when and where they matter most.

Class of 2019, you have used those talents well in your years here at UT. The world needs your talents now. The world needs you now. The eyes of Texas and the world are upon you. So, step up... and take risks. Because the rewards—for you and the lives you change—will be worth it. Congratulations and hook 'em horns!" (Dell, 2019)

MARK ZUCKERBERG
Co-founder of Facebook, Inc., chairman, CEO, and controlling shareholder

Project with purpose.

"President Faust, Board of Overseers, faculty, alumni, friends, proud parents, members of the ad board, and graduates of the greatest university in the world.

I'm honored to be with you today because, let's face it, you accomplished something I never could. If I get through this speech, it'll be the first time I actually finish something at Harvard. Class of 2017, congratulations!

I'm an unlikely speaker, not just because I dropped out, but because we're technically in the same generation. We walked this yard less than a decade apart, studied the same ideas and slept through the same Ec10 lectures. We may have taken different paths to get here, especially if you came all the way from the Quad, but today I want to share what I've learned about our generation and the world we're building together.

But first, the last couple of days have brought back a lot of good memories.

How many of you remember exactly what you were doing when you got that email telling you that you got into Harvard? I was playing Civilization and I ran downstairs, got my dad, and for some reason, his reaction was to video me opening the email. That could have been a really sad video. I swear getting into Harvard is still the thing my parents are most proud of me for.

What about your first lecture at Harvard? Mine was Computer Science 121 with the incredible Harry Lewis. I was late so I threw on a t-shirt and didn't realize until afterwards it was inside out and backwards with my tag sticking out the front. I couldn't figure out why no one would talk to me — except one guy, KX Jin, he just went with it. We ended up doing our problem sets together, and now he runs a big part of Facebook. And that, Class of 2017, is why you should be nice to people.

But my best memory from Harvard was meeting Priscilla. I had just launched this prank website Facemash, and the ad board wanted to "see me". Everyone thought I was going to get kicked out. My parents came to help me pack. My friends threw me a going away party. As luck would have it, Priscilla was at that party with her friend. We met in line for the bathroom in the Pooh Belltower, and in what must be one of the all-time romantic lines, I said: "I'm going to get kicked out in three days, so we need to go on a date quickly."

Actually, any of you graduating can use that line.

I didn't end up getting kicked out — I did that to myself. Priscilla and I started dating. And, you know, that movie made it seem like Facemash was so important to creating Facebook. It wasn't. But without Facemash I wouldn't have met Priscilla, and she's the most important person in my life, so you could say it was the most important thing I built in my time here.

We've all started lifelong friendships here, and some of us even families. That's why I'm so grateful to this place. Thanks, Harvard.

Today I want to talk about purpose. But I'm not here to give you the standard commencement about finding your purpose. We're millennials. We'll try to do that instinctively. Instead, I'm here to tell you finding your purpose isn't enough. The challenge for our generation is creating a world where everyone has a sense of purpose.

One of my favorite stories is when John F Kennedy visited the NASA space center, he saw a janitor carrying a broom and he walked over and asked what he was doing. The janitor responded: "Mr. President, I'm helping put a man on the moon".

Purpose is that sense that we are part of something bigger than ourselves, that we are needed, that we have something better ahead to work for. Purpose is what creates true happiness.

You're graduating at a time when this is especially important. When our parents graduated, purpose reliably came from your job, your church, your community. But today, technology and automation are eliminating many jobs. Membership in communities is declining. Many people feel disconnected and depressed, and are trying to fill a void.

As I've traveled around, I've sat with children in juvenile detention and opioid addicts, who told me their lives could have turned out differently if they just had something to do, an after-school program or somewhere to go. I've met factory workers who know their old jobs aren't coming back and are trying to find their place.

To keep our society moving forward, we have a generational challenge — to not only create new jobs, but create a renewed sense of purpose.

I remember the night I launched Facebook from my little dorm in Kirkland House. I went to Noch's with my friend KX. I remember telling him I was excited to connect the Harvard community, but one day someone would connect the whole world.

The thing is, it never even occurred to me that someone might be us. We were just college kids. We didn't know anything about that. There were all these big technology companies with resources. I just assumed one of them would do it. But this idea was so clear to us — that all people want to connect. So, we just kept moving forward, day by day.

I know a lot of you will have your own stories just like this. A change in the world that seems so clear you're sure someone else will do it. But they won't. You will.

But it's not enough to have purpose yourself. You have to create a sense of purpose for others.

I found that out the hard way. You see, my hope was never to build a company, but to make an impact. And as all these people started joining us, I just assumed that's what they cared about too, so I never explained what I hoped we'd build.

A couple years in, some big companies wanted to buy us. I didn't want to sell. I wanted to see if we could connect more people. We were building the first News Feed, and I thought if we could just launch this, it could change how we learn about the world.

Nearly everyone else wanted to sell. Without a sense of higher purpose, this was the startup dream come true. It tore our company apart. After one tense argument, an advisor told me if I didn't agree to sell, I would regret the decision for the rest of my life. Relationships were so frayed that within a year or so every single person on the management team was gone.

That was my hardest time leading Facebook. I believed in what we were doing, but I felt alone. And worse, it was my fault. I wondered if I was just wrong, an imposter, a 22-year-old kid who had no idea how the world worked.

Now, years later, I understand that *is* how things work with no sense of higher purpose. It's up to us to create it so we can all keep moving forward together.

Today I want to talk about three ways to create a world where everyone has a sense of purpose: by taking on big meaningful projects together, by redefining equality so everyone has the freedom to pursue purpose, and by building community across the world.

First, let's take on big meaningful projects.

Our generation will have to deal with tens of millions of jobs replaced by automation like self-driving cars and trucks. But we have the potential to do so much more together.

Every generation has its defining works. More than 300,000 people worked to put a man on the moon – including that janitor. Millions of volunteers immunized children around the world against polio. Millions of more people built the Hoover dam and other great projects.

These projects didn't just provide purpose for the people doing those jobs, they gave our whole country a sense of pride that we could do great things.

Now it's our turn to do great things. I know, you're probably thinking: I don't know how to build a dam, or get a million people involved in anything.

But let me tell you a secret: no one does when they begin. Ideas don't come out fully formed. They only become clear as you work on them. You just have to get started.

If I had to understand everything about connecting people before I began, I never would have started Facebook.

Movies and pop culture get this all wrong. The idea of a single eureka moment is a dangerous lie. It makes us feel inadequate since we haven't had ours. It prevents people with seeds of good ideas from getting started. Oh, you know what else movies get wrong about innovation? No one writes math formulas on glass. That's not a thing.

It's good to be idealistic. But be prepared to be misunderstood. Anyone working on a big vision will get called crazy, even if you end up right. Anyone working on a complex problem will get blamed for not fully understanding the challenge, even though it's impossible to know everything upfront. Anyone taking initiative will get criticized for moving too fast, because there's always someone who wants to slow you down.

In our society, we often don't do big things because we're so afraid of making mistakes that we ignore all the things wrong today if we do nothing. The reality is, anything we do will have issues in the future. But that can't keep us from starting.

So, what are we waiting for? It's time for our generation-defining public works. How about stopping climate change before we destroy the planet and getting millions of people involved manufacturing and installing solar panels? How about curing all diseases and asking volunteers to track their health data and share their genomes? Today we spend 50x more treating people who are sick than we spend finding cures so people don't get sick in the first place. That makes no sense. We can fix this. How about modernizing democracy so everyone can vote online, and personalizing education so everyone can learn?

These achievements are within our reach. Let's do them all in a way that gives everyone in our society a role. Let's do big things, not only to create progress, but to create purpose.

So, taking on big meaningful projects is the first thing we can do to create a world where everyone has a sense of purpose.

The second is redefining equality to give everyone the freedom they need to pursue purpose.

Many of our parents had stable jobs throughout their careers. Now we're all entrepreneurial, whether we're starting projects or finding or role. And that's great. Our culture of entrepreneurship is how we create so much progress.

Now, an entrepreneurial culture thrives when it's easy to try lots of new ideas. Facebook wasn't the first thing I built. I also built games, chat systems, study tools and music players. I'm not alone. JK Rowling got rejected 12 times before publishing Harry Potter. Even Beyonce had to make hundreds of songs to get Halo. The greatest successes come from having the freedom to fail.

But today, we have a level of wealth inequality that hurts everyone. When you don't have the freedom to take your idea and turn it into a historic enterprise, we all lose. Right now, our society is way over-indexed on rewarding success and we don't do nearly enough to make it easy for everyone to take lots of shots.

Let's face it. There is something wrong with our system when I can leave here and make billions of dollars in 10 years while millions of students can't afford to pay off their loans, let alone start a business.

Look, I know a lot of entrepreneurs, and I don't know a single person who gave up on starting a business because they might not make enough money. But I know lots of people who haven't pursued dreams because they didn't have a cushion to fall back on if they failed.

We all know we don't succeed just by having a good idea or working hard. We succeed by being lucky too. If I had to support my family growing up instead of having time to code, if I didn't know I'd be fine if Facebook didn't work out, I wouldn't be standing here today. If we're honest, we all know how much luck we've had.

Every generation expands its definition of equality. Previous generations fought for the vote and civil rights. They had the New Deal and Great Society. Now it's our time to define a new social contract for our generation.

We should have a society that measures progress not just by economic metrics like GDP, but by how many of us have a role we find meaningful. We should explore ideas like universal basic income to give everyone a cushion to try new things. We're going to change jobs many times, so we need affordable childcare to get to work and healthcare that aren't tied to one company. We're all going to make mistakes, so we need a society that focuses less on locking us up or stigmatizing us. And as technology keeps changing, we need to focus more on continuous education throughout our lives.

And yes, giving everyone the freedom to pursue purpose isn't free. People like me should pay for it. Many of you will do well and you should too.

That's why Priscilla and I started the Chan Zuckerberg Initiative and committed our wealth to promoting equal opportunity. These are the values of our generation. It was never a question of if we were going to do this. The only question was when.

Millennials are already one of the most charitable generations in history. In one year, three of four US millennials made a donation and seven out of ten raised money for charity.

But it's not just about money. You can also give time. I promise you, if you take an hour or two a week — that's all it takes to give someone a hand, to help them reach their potential.

Maybe you think that's too much time. I used to. When Priscilla graduated from Harvard, she became a teacher, and before she'd do education work with me, she told me I needed to teach a class. I complained: "Well, I'm kind of busy. I'm running this company." But she insisted, so I taught a middle school program on entrepreneurship at the local Boys and Girls Club.

I taught them lessons on product development and marketing, and they taught me what it's like feeling targeted for your race and having a family member in prison. I shared stories from my time in school, and they shared their hope of one day going to college too. For five years now, I've been having dinner with those kids every month. One of them threw me and Priscilla our first baby shower. And next year they're going to college. Every one of them. First in their families.

We can all make time to give someone a hand. Let's give everyone the freedom to pursue their purpose — not only because it's the right thing to do, but because when more people can turn their dreams into something great, we're all better for it.

Purpose doesn't only come from work. The third way we can create a sense of purpose for everyone is by building community. And when our generation says "everyone", we mean everyone in the world.

Quick show of hands: how many of you are from another country? Now, how many of you are friends with one of these folks? Now we're talking. We have grown up connected.

In a survey asking millennials around the world what defines our identity, the most popular answer wasn't nationality, religion or ethnicity, it was "citizen of the world". That's a big deal.

Every generation expands the circle of people we consider "one of us". For us, it now encompasses the entire world.

We understand the great arc of human history bends towards people coming together in ever greater numbers — from tribes to cities to nations — to achieve things we couldn't on our own.

We get that our greatest opportunities are now global — we can be the generation that ends poverty, that ends disease. We get that our greatest challenges need global responses too — no country can fight climate change alone or prevent pandemics. Progress now requires coming together not just as cities or nations, but also as a global community.

But we live in an unstable time. There are people left behind by globalization across the world. It's hard to care about people in other places if we don't feel good about our lives here at home. There's pressure to turn inwards.

This is the struggle of our time. The forces of freedom, openness and global community against the forces of authoritarianism, isolationism and nationalism. Forces for the flow of knowledge, trade and immigration against those who would slow them down. This is not a battle of nations, it's a battle of ideas. There are people in every country for global connection and good people against it.

This isn't going to be decided at the UN either. It's going to happen at the local level, when enough of us feel a sense of purpose and stability in our own lives that we can open up and start caring about everyone. The best way to do that is to start building local communities right now.

We all get meaning from our communities. Whether our communities are houses or sports teams, churches or music groups, they give us that sense we are part of something bigger, that we are not alone; they give us the strength to expand our horizons.

That's why it's so striking that for decades, membership in all kinds of groups has declined as much as one-quarter. That's a lot of people who now need to find purpose somewhere else.

But I know we can rebuild our communities and start new ones because many of you already are.

I met Agnes Igoye, who's graduating today. Where are you, Agnes? She spent her childhood navigating conflict zones in Uganda, and now she trains thousands of law enforcement officers to keep communities safe.

I met Kayla Oakley and Niha Jain, graduating today, too. Stand up. Kayla and Niha started a non-profit that connects people suffering from illnesses with people in their communities willing to help.

I met David Razu Aznar, graduating from the Kennedy School today. David, stand up. He's a former city councilor who successfully led the battle to make Mexico City the first Latin American city to pass marriage equality — even before San Francisco.

This is my story too. A student in a dorm room, connecting one community at a time, and keeping at it until one day we connect the whole world.

Change starts local. Even global changes start small — with people like us. In our generation, the struggle of whether we connect more, whether we achieve our biggest opportunities, comes down to this — your ability to build communities and create a world where every single person has a sense of purpose.

Class of 2017, you are graduating into a world that needs purpose. It's up to you to create it.

Now, you may be thinking: can I really do this?

Remember when I told you about that class I taught at the Boys and Girls Club? One day after class I was talking to them about college, and one of my top students raised his hand and said he wasn't sure he could go because he's undocumented. He didn't know if they'd let him in.

Last year I took him out to breakfast for his birthday. I wanted to get him a present, so I asked him and he started talking about students he saw struggling and said "You know, I'd really just like a book on social justice."

I was blown away. Here's a young guy who has every reason to be cynical. He didn't know if the country he calls home — the only one he's known — would deny him his dream of going to college. But he wasn't feeling sorry for himself. He wasn't even thinking of himself. He has a greater sense of purpose, and he's going to bring people along with him.

It says something about our current situation that I can't even say his name because I don't want to put him at risk. But if a high school senior who doesn't know what the future holds can do his part to move the world forward, then we owe it to the world to do our part too.

Before you walk out those gates one last time, as we sit in front of Memorial Church, I am reminded of a prayer, Mi Shebeirach, that I say whenever I face a challenge, that I sing to my daughter thinking about her future when I tuck her into bed. It goes:

"May the source of strength, who blessed the ones before us, help us *find the courage* to make our lives a blessing."

I hope you find the courage to make your life a blessing.

Congratulations, Class of '17! Good luck out there." (Zuckerberg, 2017)

ERICK SCHMIDT
CEO of Google and President of Alphabet Inc.

Adore life.

"Thank you. Well thank you all. It's great to be here, and it's an honor to have been invited. It's an honor to look out on the next generation of BU Terriers. Now let me give you a quote: "I am a true adorer of life, and if I can't reach as high as the face of it, I plant my kiss somewhere lower down. Those who understand will require no further explanation."

Well, graduates, now let me to explain. You used to have a professor here — a decent writer by the name of Saul Bellow. And this comes from his novel "Henderson and the Rain King." And I stand before you today as someone who considers himself an adorer of life. I know what it's like to plant a kiss on a life lived fully, and I can tell you from experience that, once you understand that, Professor Bellow's right: that no further explanation is necessary. Live it to the full.

It's one quote from countless beautiful lines he wrote over his career. But I feel it best sums up an approach that contains the power to transform an ordinary life into one filled with grace and love and dignity.

And it also best, in my view, sums up what a fantastic university like BU tries to inculcate in every one of you who sets foot on this beautiful campus. And you just look at that. And scientists, engineers, writers, business pioneers, governors, Olympic gold medalists, Oscar winners, cabinet secretaries, they all walked across this stage and left their mark on the culture, on society, and on the world.

And, my God, even Martin Luther King is Doctor King because of the PhD that he got here. Pretty amazing. And now you follow. You right, sitting there now, baking in the sun, thinking about the Celtics game tomorrow, possibly nursing a hangover — there's one down here I've been watching — saying to yourself — she knows who she is — "Wow, that's a lot of pressure. What can I do?" "Where can I plant my kiss?"

Well, that's your question to answer. I can't do it for you. But what I know, is I know one thing for certain: No graduating class gets to choose the world they graduate into — just as you can't choose your siblings and your parents. Welcome to them too of course.

Now every class has its own unique challenges. Every class enters a history that, up to that point, is being written for it. This is no different.

What is different, though, is the chance that each generation has to make history and to make it larger or, in my business, to program it better. And, on that score, your generation's opportunities are greater than any generation's in modern history. You can write the code for all of us. You're connecting to each other in ways those who came before you could never dream of. And you're using these connections to strengthen the invisible ties that hold humanity together, and to deepen our understanding of the world around us. You are emblems of the sense of possibility that will define this new age.

In the past, it's always been older generations, standing up on high, trying to teach the next generation the ways of the world — you know how it goes — trying to make sure they follow in their footsteps.

Well, graduates, I think it's different today. You are teaching us. Interesting. This generation — your generation — is the first fully connected generation the world has ever known.

What's the first thing that you guys do when you wake up? Right? Check your phone? Your laptop? Read some email, comb through your social networks? "I'm awake! Here I am!" If you're awake, you're online. You're connected. Some of you are probably texting right now or tweeting this speech. Changing your status, smiling. "Here we are, smile, you're on camera."

There's this joke, by the way, about the college kid getting mugged, who says, "Hold on, hold on, I need to update my status, telling my friends that now I'm getting mugged, then I'll give you my phone."

Now obviously — well, it actually did happen, but this is a stark depiction of how just essential technology has become to your generation's identity and your ability to connect with the world.

Identity and connection — concepts as old as humanity itself — they make up so much of what we are, who we are now. They shape the things the way they are today, they define the human condition.

Identity and connection — it is your task to take these timeworn concepts, spin them around, reinvigorate them, make them fresh and new and exciting. And you can do this.

Now BU has built the platform that you can do this on. I know it's daunting. It's not a great economy to be walking off this stage into. I know all of this. But you have an advantage, you have a competitive edge. You have an innate mastery of technology, an ability to find, build and foster connections that no generation before you have ever possessed. It's a very, very powerful skill that you taught yourself.

People bemoan this generation that is growing up living life in front of screens, always connected to something or someone. These people are wrong. They are absolutely wrong. The fact that we are all connected now is a blessing, not a curse, and we can solve many problems in the world as a result. Not only is it an advantage you have; it's a responsibility that you carry.

Today, there are 54 wars and conflicts going around. It's terrible. 1.5 billion people live on less than $1 a day, and hundreds of millions of children go to bed hungry tonight. It's terrible. Nearly half the world's people don't live under democratic governments — the rights that we all enjoy are a rarity, they're not the norm.

And when it comes to the Internet, we think everyone else is online because all of us are online all now. But only 1 billion people have smartphones, and only 2 billion people are connected to the web. For most of the world, the internet cafes and all that kind of stuff that we take for granted are far-off digital oases in technology wastelands. They don't have access to it.

But in this century – your century, not mine — there is a chance for change on the horizon. The spread of mobile phones, the new forms of connectivity, offer the prospect of connecting everybody. And when that happens, connectivity will revolutionize every aspect of society — politically, socially, economically. To connect the world is to free the world, I say.

And if we get this right, then we can fix all the world's most pressing problems, to beam bright rays of hope to millions who can see it as only a flicker. You have that power, right in your pockets or your pocketbooks, right now.

And here's the deal: Yes, I know — we all have this knowledge literally at our fingertips. But, now just as we know more than we used to doesn't mean our problems just go away. The future doesn't just happen. It's not etched or written or coded somewhere. There's no algorithm or formula that says something will do X or Y will be sure to occur. Technology doesn't work on its own. It's a tool. You are the ones who harness that power. And that requires innovation and entrepreneurship.

Innovation is disruptive; one thing I'll tell you: you know you are innovating when people are worried about you. Graduates, please make people worry — not your parents, but everybody else.

Entrepreneurship is the lifeblood of a new economy. It's a more prosperous society – the engine that keeps communities growing. Two-thirds of the new jobs created are in small businesses, and you all should try to create a small business, or be part of one and, of course, I would recommend that you use all the products that Google has to offer to set it up. End of that.

Now you all have a chance to make an original contribution. Don't just be a shepherd following somebody else's vision and ideas — new models, new forms, new thinking — that's what we need from you. You don't need to become an aid worker or a teacher although, that's obviously good. You don't need to be an engineer, I obviously like that, right, we love this. Everyone — all of you — can make your mark by creating new standards of brilliance and innovation. And, those standards can spread. They can scale. They can scale in ways that are once unimaginable.

The collective intelligence of our society, our version of the Borg, is really quite different. Think of this as a new society, with shared norms and values, that crosses continents and unites all of us. The empowerment of each of us empowers all of us; and the distinctive feature of your new world – the distinctive feature is that you can be unique while being completely connected. It's never been possible before. I think this is the true fulfillment of the American Dream.

You see, computers can do amazing things. Those things in your pockets — they contain power inside them that your proud parents, your grandparents in the audience never could have possibly imagined. I certainly didn't. These computers, they have speed. They have memory. They have intricately complicated wiring and unfathomably complex circuitry.

But there's one thing that they don't have: They don't have a heart. All of these connections that you forge, all the things that I'm talking about — the digital ties that bind our humanity together are not possible without technology. But it's also not possible without you, without a heart. You have the heart. And the future will not beat without you.

Now, don't get me wrong. I obviously believe fully in the power of technology to change the world for the better. Obviously. And I believe even more fully in the ability of your generation to use that power to great effect — to rule technology. But you can't let technology rule you.

Remember — and I want you to remember this — the one thing you have to remember from my talk: I want you to take one hour a day and turn that thing off. I know it's going to be hard. I know it's going to be hard. I want you to take one hour - just one hour - you do the math, it's 1/24th. Turn it down. Shut it off. Shut it down. Learn where the OFF button is. Take your eyes off that screen, and look into the eyes of the person that you love. Have a conversation — a real conversation — with the friends who make you think, with the family who make you laugh.

Don't push a button saying I "Like" something. Actually, tell them. What a concept! Engage in the world around you, and feel and taste and smell and hug what's there, right in front of you — not what's a click away. Life is not lived in the glow of a monitor. Life is not a series of status updates. Life is not about your friend count, it's about the friends you can actually count on.

So, life is about who you love, how you live, it's about who you travel through the world with. Your family, your collaborators, your friends. Life is a social experience first, and the best aspects of that experience are not lonely ones — they are spent in the company of others.

Now it's okay after that hour to turn it back on. Our modern landscape has changed, yes — but our humanity will always remain, and that, above all else, is what makes us who we are. And who you are, is a proud and talented group of BU Terriers.

Here you have come to know extraordinary people. Look around, take a minute. A few years ago, you started off on the road here with these people, knowing them as boys and girls, running around campus, dazed and overwhelmed. Now you are extraordinary men and women, in total control of your destinies, ready to make your mark not on history but on the future.

And the friendships that you forged when the times were good, and when the ones they were bad — and when you realized you overslept your lecture and needed someone's notes to catch up with, and all the other stuff that goes on in college — those are the friendships that will matter for your whole life. The people you have met here will be some of the strongest friends and closest allies you will ever meet in your lives. It's been that way certainly for me.

When you leave here, don't leave them behind. Don't leave BU behind. Don't leave them behind. Stay close and stay strong. Take them with you wherever you go, and, together, connected, go and change the world with all the things we've talked about.

At times it may have seemed like the road ahead was an impossible slog. But today, I have the distinct honor of telling you: you have made it. You only have another half-hour to go! It's incredible.

Now that you're here, I want you do to another thing: I ask each of you – I want you to find a way to say "Yes" to things. Say "yes" to invitations, to a new country, say "yes" to meet new friends, say "yes" to learning a new language, and picking up a new sport. "Yes" is how you get your first job, and your next job. "Yes" is how you find your spouse, and even your children. And even if it is a bit edgy, a bit out of your comfort zone, saying "yes" means that you will do something new, meet someone new, and make a difference in your life and likely in other people's as well.

"Yes" lets you stand out in a crowd, to be an optimist, to stay positive, to be the one that everyone comes to for help, for advice, or just for fun. "Yes" is what keeps us all young. "Yes" is a tiny word that can do very big things. And say it often.

Second thing I want you to do: Do not be afraid to fail, but also do not be afraid to succeed. There's an old Italian phrase that I like. It's used to describe especially daring circus performers — they do the *salto mortale*. It means they do a somersault, on a tightrope, without a net. Graduates, you need to do this. Be brave. Work without a net. I promise you; you will land on your feet.

For those who say that you're thinking too big, be smart enough not to listen. For those who say that the odds are too small, be dumb enough to give it a shot.

And for those who ask, how could I do that? look them straight in the eyes and say, "I will figure it out."

But above all, be an "adorer of life." I don't think any further explanation is necessary.

I, to be very clear, am very happy to have you join us as adults, and the quicker we have you lead, the better. Time to throw out all of us aging baby boomers and replace it by those best-equipped to lead us into a new age — you. March us to a better day.

The power and the possibility, the intellectual energy and the human electricity seated in this stadium, which I see in front of me and this is happening in other stadiums around this weekend and next weekend, this generation will break a new day. Your vast knowledge will seed a new era. Your new ideas will shape a new reality. Your agile minds will shape a new dawn. You will give our future a heartbeat. And that beat will be stronger, because of you, because of the things you learn, and the things that you care about and the values, and the things that you're going to do.

From my perspective looking at this class, I say that you have the potential to reach higher than any class before you, than any generation that ever came before you. You can reach as high as the face of life itself.

I want to thank you all for listening to me, and my sincere congratulations to every single one of you, and your families. It's a great day.

Thank you so much." (Schmidt, 2012)

Adding the Grenadine syrup on business
Design

Being good in business is the most fascinating kind of art
ANDY WARHOL
American artist of the visual art movement, pop art

As the third ingredient of this combined classic, its work is to detonate the impact with which materialize the experience of your business. Its specific management, is to facilitate the active substance to communicate forceful as a visual reflection of your product, in order to project the effect of your business and stay in the mind of your consumer.

To give effect to business, you need to the design and is extremely important to keep in mind its definition.

Zimmermann (1998) states that, "particle 'de' of design word comes from Greek *dia* which means divided, twice, which belongs to; the word 'sign' comes from the Latin *signa, signum*, and means signal, mark, insignia, ensign, flag, that is, design means 'belonging to the sign.' Latin *designare*, meaning mark, draw, designate; generates the Italian *disegnare* and the term *disegno.*" "Design" in English.

Dondis (1992) says that when analyzing the visual expression as a communication resource, certifies that the product of a highly complex human intelligence, which is a whole body of data that can be used to compose and understand messages located at very different levels of utility, from the purely functional to the highest artistic expressions, so the design is the composition process the verbal and the visual in a direct transmission of information, with the possibility that a design professional contribute innovations in many levels visual expression.

Meanwhile Wong (1995) states that a good and faithful and effectively forming design aesthetic and functional, is the best visual expression of the essence of an object, a message or a product, it must meet the needs of a consumer by a graphic design unit placed in front of the public eye and convey a message, to manufacture, distribute, use and relate to their environment, while reflecting or guide the taste of his time. If the design in addition to beautify the outward appearance of things, is a process of visual creation has a purpose: Cover demands practices wearer.

In this regard Zimmermann (1998) points out that specifically design are the objective and rational criteria configuration of an object and its image since the most basic reason and the primary purpose of a design object intended to solve the problems of the human being is: its use, its usefulness.

According to Bonsiepe (1999) the full realization of design requires an interface, the space that articulates the interaction between a user, task and utensil in other words, that we need a field of action where the constitution is projected between the human body, the object of an action and a device or information in the field of communicative action, to transform them to form a unit or a utensil connotation, not only formal and aesthetic, but legitimate. There, in the space of human action, is where is located the inalienable domain design and where is oriented designer interest.

Where warns not to fall into the unfounded generalization of "everything is design" since not all are designers, because the term refers to a potential. Although it states than by manifest itself in the discovery, everyone has access to it and everyone can become designers in the field of discipline if the area in which to develop their project activity is perfectly defined.

Much so that an employer, or a director when conducting your business in a new way, makes design; an engineer who conceived a method, or develop a new feature, is doing design. Where the project is a core activity for all human activities and professions, and its contents are not limited to material products.

In this context, defines the design as a special mode of action innovative and focused on a concern in charge of the needs of users.

And refers to a reinterpretation of the design of seven characteristics regardless of the framework of good design:

1. It is a domain that can manifest in all fields of human activity.
2. It is oriented toward the future.

3.   Refers to innovation. The act of projecting brings to the world something new.

4.   It is referred to the body and space, especially the visual space.

5.   It points to effective action.

6.   Linguistically it is anchored in the field of the judgments.

7.   He heads for the interaction between the user and the artifact. The design domain is the domain of the interface.

To expand the concept, Chaves (2001) founded that the evolution of the visual arts and their application in industry, design the first decades twentieth century appears as a transformative force that is not strictly limited to production, technical and aesthetic aspects, the design comes loaded with a desire for social transformation. Now, design has shown great participation as a necessary element between society and business, has been present in increasingly competitive markets, the consumer requires the design, not only as a value added to a product but as a product.

In this sense Chaves stresses that it is important to highlight the universality of three of the manifestations occurred in the discourse of design:

The market discourse: where business and corporate agents are constituted linked to the development of markets, which is essential to address the needs of the consumer; business management, marketing and design competitiveness. That is precisely that the business strategy adopted the design make product improvements based on their innovations aimed at satisfying consumption.

The discourse of the founders of design: in which it is constitutes an ideology of social agents in which, attend to user relations, social phenomena, visual grammar and cultural vanguards, it is an obligation. That defines the purpose of design optimize communication functions and their use in the rational development of any project, to satisfy the needs of use.

The post-vanguard discourse is not so different from the first, except that it is now an ideology that rescues the high values of the cultural elites of discipline and sets off with the values of the indispensable market demands.

Based on the work of designers Tibor Kalman and Oliviero Toscani in the magazine Colors of Benetton, O'Reilly (2002) summarizes the design achieves a visual object containing a narrative through images, not only to communicate messages, show ideas and sell products, but to be useful to get people to think into images and on them.

In the words of Joan Costa, "the design serves to make the world intelligible to improve the lives of people and to make it understandable our environment, among other things. Will ultimately, the design is a powerful communication tool."

Basic concept: The design process formulates the beginning of the project, different stages of development and analysis of results. Bring a large control planning, implementation and review. All aspects of creation.

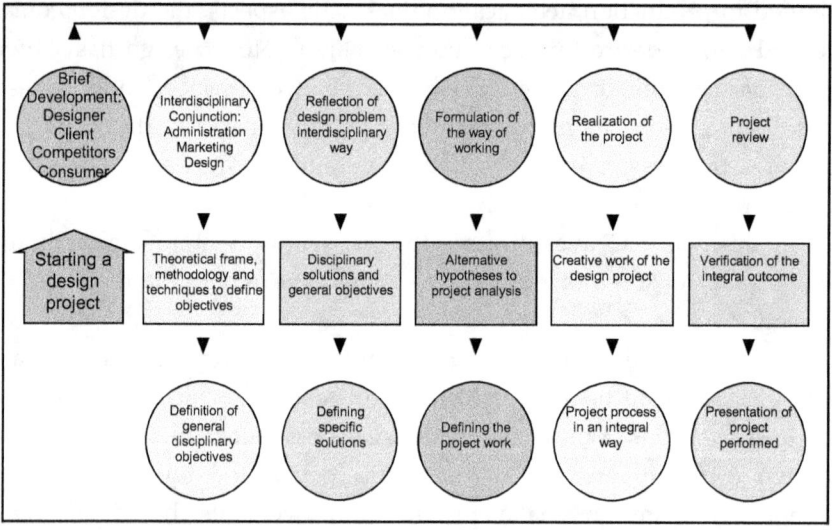

The design process. Adapted from: Rodríguez Morales, Luis. *Para una teoría del diseño*. [For a theory of design]. Mexico: Tilde-UAM Azcapotzalco, 1989. 125 pp. p. 42.

Fundamentals of design and product

The design is a language and the main thing is how you use that language
TIBOR KALMAN
Hungarian graphic designer

Hauser (1978) mentions that since its origins the human being has yearned to express its nature and understanding of the world. During the Neolithic, between 7000 and 4000 B.C. everywhere the first rupestrian art produced geometrically stylized images, ideographic, schematic and conventional signs that indicate more than reproduce the object.

According to Gombrich (1999) for the IV millennium BC born in Sumerian cuneiform script, and 2600 BC heraldry develops precise and symmetrical. Too since the third millennium B.C. between 2750 and 1900 B.C. mural painting and Egyptian hieroglyphic writing highlighted in narrative-descriptive altarpieces, where it was not the most important beauty but perfection.

Satué (1988) shows that in the last 2500 years various technologies have been used to express and communicate through images, at the same time the sense that recover the images has been enriched based on constant processes that formulate the theoretical platform and fundamental practices builders of graphic design.

• In Rome from 27 B.C. to 330 A.D. produce images symbolic information and use the icons as distinguishing marks.

• In the Middle Ages images produce cult in themselves and is given admiration the visual arts of the aristocratic elite.

• In the High Middle Ages XV century, the xylograph was used, a mechanical recorder that tills their wooden planks to pamphlets few leaves.

• In the Renaissance the images are considered fetishes or sacred ideas; It inform with the use of the cards and Bibles to the lower class, is achieved the correct building types the graphics architecture and xylography records the first impression in series.

• From 1440 to 1500 are developed first typographical printed books, Constance Missal and the 42-line Bible, of metal movable type by Johan Gutenberg.

- Towards the end of the XVIII century in England design is brewing as we know it today with the Industrial Revolution.
- In 1785 The Times newspaper is the first epoch header graphic and the American Type Founders Company in New York is at the peak of its inception.
- In 1796 Alois Senefelder invents in Munich the lithographer, mechanical engraver who tills their plates in stone; lithography meant procedure for applying color.
- In the XIX century London and Paris develops commercial graphic design. At the end of the century, in Great Britain an effort was made to divide the Fine Arts and Applied Arts.
- In 1884 with Ottmar Mergenthaler develops Linotype.
- In 1866 begins the use of advertising, United States uses naturally and mimicry, the drive industrial companies in 1886 Coca Cola, Pepsi in 1898, Mercedes Benz and Ford in 1900, in 1908 Pirelli, Michelin in 1910 and 1914 Camel.
- From 1912 graphics design serves to trade and industry, decade in which political poster war begins, and advertising continues.
- Since 1918 starts building the graphic design with the strength of the Bauhaus; in 1928 advertising loses strength and is until 1932 when the design is established as a profession.
- By 1974 graphic design extends maturity and develops its identity in the United States and Latin America.

From the evolutionary result of visual arts becomes a wise use of their communication elements. Then the design begins to produce in series and to have a social utility. This trajectory as ideologies have formed the artistic vanguards that support graphic design, wrought as discipline that works in industry, science, consumerism and global approaches.

Kunst (1995) elucidates that in the early twentieth century graphic design was used to educate the working class, at the same time, tradition, expertise and existing freedom given the opportunity to develop a graphic design style characterized by individualism. Now simply accepting current fashions devastates creativity; man, as a designer should start thinking seriously about his craft since he began his studies, reflection is part of their activity. Who designs requires not only talent to graph but the capacity for analysis, reflection, research and ideology to provide the image and its context of a proper sense should know submit their intentions to the intellect to reasonably ensure the viability of their project.

Grefé (1997) accurate to the American Institute of Graphic Arts [AIGA] leader institution in the provision of knowledge sharing ideas and information, in its publication "The Culture of Design," an anthology of writings of graphic design journal AIGA, dedicated to the progress of excellence in graphic design, in his article: is design important? He defines it as a discipline, a profession and a cultural force. Also, as an organization that promotes critical analysis and research on the educational progress of design and its ethical practice, provides the essentials to be considered for projecting within the professional circles of graphic design.

Joan Costa, cited by Guyot in the journal *La Nación* (2008) affirm that although the role of design is to solve communication problems, its reductionism to embellish things only makes it lose part of their communicative force however the aesthetic component is always part of their message. "A designer it does is communicating, creating a message for the eyes and mind. A message should be fundamentally considered the recipient... The design must to scramble to the culture, education for citizenship. Because the current design has plenty of technology and lacks methodology and philosophy."

That is why according to Gunnar Swanson (in Grefé, 1997) within the discipline is an obligation reflect on our education and approach to other disciplines that integrate traditional knowledge areas, which similarly are used in the realization of a design project, pretending the design as a study area where manufacturing knows philosophy and so have development in today's professional environment because design practice is linked to business and interact in these firmly. On the other hand, interest in the business of design also has its tradition in education. Without such a balance of forces design and design business are in trouble.

Thereon Frías (2004) in this way concludes that it is clear that the stages in which the design has participated and has impacted the development of humanity are constant, in technological terms the Industrial Revolution is one of them, in the academic the Bauhaus; This German School motivated and educated its students towards the creation of a work to be produced in series and to have a social utility theory valid and in force to this day.

For his intellectual trajectory, their vanguards in history and its role in business, design is a discipline that stands on the cusp of education and professional development.

Basic concept: Professionalism in design is essential, involves understanding requirements throughout the design process for success in business.

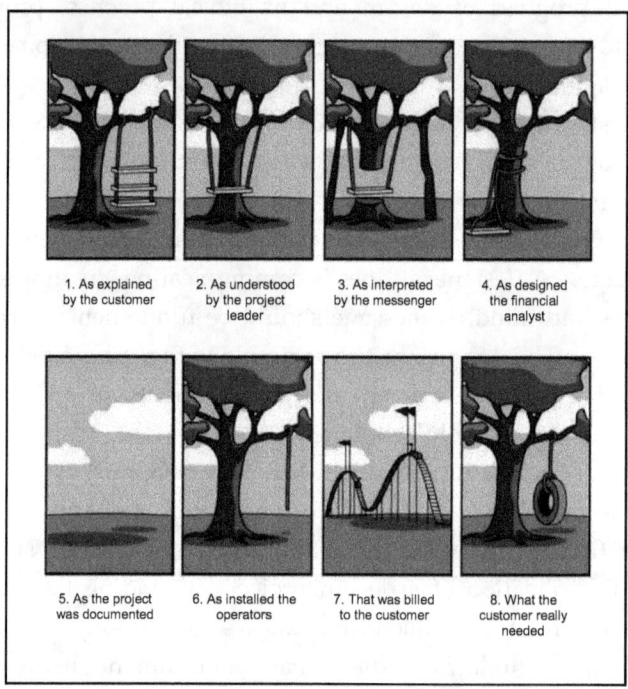

"How not to design a swing." Adapted from: University of London. *Acknowledgment to unknown author*. Newsletter. March 1973. N°. 53. http://i0.kym-cdn.com/photos/images/newsfeed/000/475/752/25a.jpg Also: Mike Smith. *a! Diseño*. [a! Diseño magazine] 12, (67). p. 57. And: https://www.webdesign.tm/

The intent of the design philosophy

The design is intelligence that identifies things
OSCAR MARINÉ
Spanish designer, illustrator, typographer and artist

According to Satué (1988) art movements of end of century XIX and early XX century and the political turmoil that accompanied them, generated dramatic changes in graphic design. Cubism (1908) Futurism (1909), Suprematism (1915) Constructivism (1915), Dada (1916), which gave way to Surrealism (1920), De Stijl (1917), Art Nouveau (1890), which evolved into Art Deco (1920) and the Bauhaus (1919), created a new vision that influenced all branches of the visual arts and design. All these movements opposed to popular decorative arts and appeared with a revisionist and transgressive spirit in all artistic activities of the time. In this period would concentrate the background of a formal and conceptual break, by which artists and educators expressed their views which fully affected the germinal construction of a more technical graphic design and disciplining.

Kunst (1995) adds that the revolutionary thought and the technical proposal of the great philosophers of the Bauhaus, the design acquired a multidisciplinary character proposed the training foundations of their practice, its application and its purpose.

The great masters of design of the twentieth century were not only able to express themselves in their craft but used the word to clarify ideas, formulate premises and generate the basic texts of what might someday become a design philosophy. The work of these designers was supported by a solid intellectual platform from where they could take off easily to areas not yet glimpsed by his contemporaries.

(Droste, 1991) and (Wingler, 1975) coincide where the design philosophy born in the German Bauhaus school of design and graphic grades which worked from 1919 to 1933, begins to merge two existing schools in the city of Weimar. It was started in Weimar from 1919 to 1925 in Dessau from 1925 to 1932 and in Berlin from 1932 to 1933. It was directed by Gropius, H. Meyer y L. Mies van der Rohe.

As the cultural center and pedagogical core of most important visual arts of the twentieth century, that school linked the rational visual arts among themselves to converge expressively in integral architecture and design of equipment.

For his part (Droste, 1991) (Lupton & Abbott, 1994) and (Satué, 1988) illustrate some of the important events in the development of design and agree that in 1919 Walter Gropius architect founder of the Bauhaus, prophesied that unified construction of Visual Arts is the ultimate objective. The first to define the term graphic design was the designer and typographer William Addison Dwiggins in 1922. Johannes Itten first professor of Basic Course at the Bauhaus, Paul Klee author of "Pedagogical Sketchbook" and Wassily Kandinsky author of "Point and line to plane" in 1923 sought the origin of visual language in basic geometries, pure color and abstraction, with a universal correspondence to each other with no graphics experiences, constituting an analysis of shapes, colors and materials. For they served as a deed with which it could be analyzed and represented the visible prehistory highlighting geometric shapes, crosslinking space and rational use of typography. Its layout is perceived as a *Gestalt* that Giorgy Kepes and Laszlo Moholy-Nagy used subsequently to provide scientific rationality to the language of vision. Herbert Bayer, who led from 1925 to 1928 the typography and advertising workshop at the Bauhaus, created the conditions for a new profession: graphic designer. He put the subject "Advertising" in the education program including, inter alia, the analysis of media advertising and Psychology of advertising. Jan Tschichold reflected the principles of modern typography in his 1928 book, New Typography. The visual form was considered as a universal scripture that spoke directly with the mechanics of the eye to the brain. This is how Tschichold, Bayer, Moholy-Nagy and Lisitski they became the parents of graphic design as we know it today. By assimilating their methods in modern design education, the Bauhaus became a point of origin which serves as an introduction to the grammar of visual writing on that the graph is a model of pictorial expression.

Satué (1988) mentions that in the mid-1950s in the United Kingdom, rose the Pop Art or Folk Art detonated later that decade in America, aspired to be the witness of the time with Jasper Johns, Andy Warhol, C. Oldenburg, George Segal, Peter Blake and Roy Lichtenstein. It was inspired by the life of the city, taking the mass culture products as elements of figurative expression and uses everyday objects of the consumer society: soda bottles, beer cans fridges, cars, comics, movie characters and music, and so on, uses Dadaists procedures (readymades), hyperrealistic (in photographic fidelity) and Cubist (with collages). Predominates in this art the colorful bright, fluorescent dyes and colorful acrylic.

Satué complements the Hochschule für Gestaltung (HfG) of Ulm was another key institution in the development of graphic design. Since its founding, distanced itself from advertising. His department was called Visual Design to solve design problems of mass communication unpersuasive, like the traffic sign systems, drawings of technical devices, or visual translation of scientific content. In the academic year 1956-1957 the name was changed to Visual Communication, based on the model of Visual Communication Department of the New Bauhaus in Chicago.

While in 1962 the official definition of the profession was directed almost exclusively to advertising activities, now extended to include areas situated under the rubric of visual communication.

O'Reilly (2002) argues that within the discipline, an example that speaks of what the place of the graphic design in society and what their philosophy is the manifesto "The first things first," which is a work that seemed to question the basic premises of graphic design presented at the Institute of Contemporary Arts in London (ICA) in 1964 by its author designer Ken Garland and written during the height of a meeting of the Society of Industrial Artists in London. In it signed graphic designers, photographers and students who disagree with those who exploit the profession to sell. The manifesto declares that is not opposed to consumer advertising itself, but wishes to tip the balance of the work performed by designers to projects with more social intentions.

Satué (1988) mentions that another notable designer is Milton Glaser who designed the unmistakable I Love NY campaign in 1973 with great success. Glaser took elements of popular culture of the sixties and seventies.

Licko (2002) as one of the first designers to exploit the potential of Apple Macintosh strongly inspired graphic design on technological advances in printing and photography since 1980 when she began creating fonts using dot matrix, made compositions of typographic design and photography, and by 1984 Zuzana Licko with her husband Rudy VanderLans founded the pioneering Emigre magazine that became the bible of digital design and took advantage of the development of Adobe and Microsoft to incorporate advanced typographic features, extending the design culture to technology and editorial design.

O'Reilly (2002) adds that little more than three decades later, the manifesto: "The first things first 2000," is as separate update as the original manifest and defends the same premises. It was signed by 33 people and was published in Adbusters, Émigré and daily AIGA in the United States; in the Eye and Blueprint magazines in the United Kingdom; and items Netherlands; I.D. and Communication Arts in the United States; Form in Germany; and Idea in Japan. Unlike the original manifesto, the latter had no direct line with the UK government, or defend any particular design style, which highlights the nature of the work done by graphic designers that has changed from the original manifest to date. Now, the discipline has been internationalized, however, has not lost its creative essence that continues to highlight to project its basic principles in the service of society.

Basic concept: A company, its brand and its products are positioned largely by the communication capability of color and his combinations, which through its visual expression has effects on the mind. Qualities: positives (+) y negatives (-).

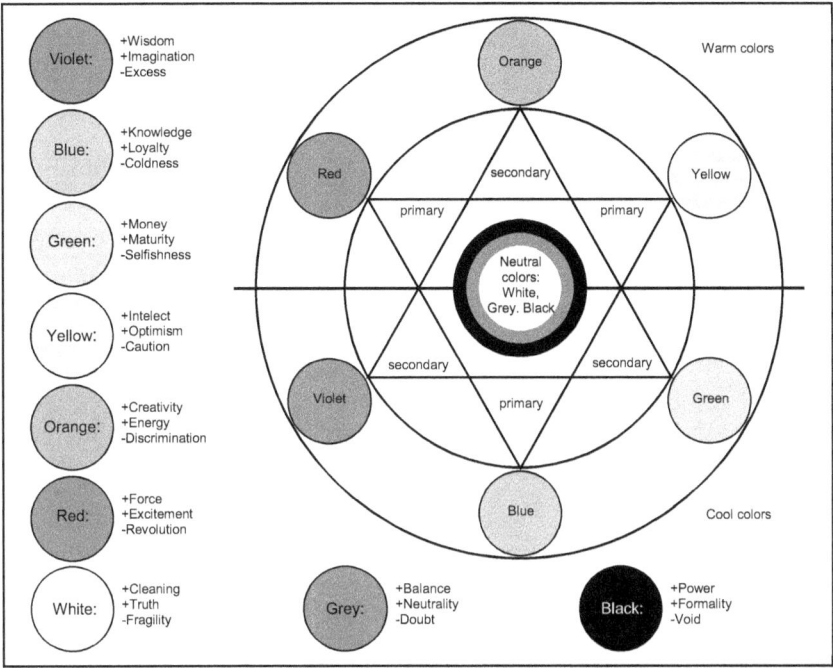

The basic color wheel and the psychology of color in products. Adapted from: Pérez Iragorri, Antonio. *a! Diseño*, [a! Diseño magazine] year 15, n°. 83, p. 59. (20-03-2007), Bimestrial, Mexico. 2007. (Grayscale representation).

Strategic design management

The product is the same, the difference lies in communication
OLIVIERO TOSCANI
Italian photographer and designer of advertising campaigns

Chaves (2001) comments that in recent decades, a large portion of graphic design work in a professional environment, have been produced in an environment of high consumption of products at the same time the little reflection of the images that the represent these representations and forms design make design practice distorted and professional awareness reduces these transformations to mere changes in language, fashion trends or the natural evolution of taste.

According to O'Reilly (2002) until now, start the XXI century, had never been so clear that the real management of graphic design and what it performed to be so ambiguous, in the era of Internet, Web pages and cheap technology design, it seems that everyone can at least pretend to be designer. If everyone can be a designer, the status of the profession and its development obviously are reduced.

The design has never been so essential for the economy since early 80s currently the design can determine a success or a commercial failure, either for a small company or a firm of international scope.

On the other hand, educational background the designer which is given imprecisely highlighting the role of design is something that remains etched in the minds of most of them. The lack of understanding toward discipline makes the definition of themselves is limited to being "creative," however this existential imperative must cope, day by day, customer demands and design processes. Note that this activity is what makes the graphic design in the most exciting way to work today because it is a discipline in which face-to-face design and business are, is converted into a milestone that marks at what point is a society.

Most of the designers negotiate in its interior the contract signed between design and money. To the outside are limited to find a point near one end or the other. Some accept tedious but well paid, jobs to work in other lower paid but most gratifying, or use the money for their own projects, the latter according to author and designer Rick Poynor is the "Robin Hood" tactic.

In this regard Wong (1995) adds that in its foundations, design as visual language is practical, what makes the designer be practical, but before facing with practical problems in professional circles, should dominate the visual language. This is the basis for creating the design that besides contain functional aspects, is driven by principles, rules and concepts of visual organization that are important to the designer and their development but working without a conscious knowledge of these, the end result of a project could reflect the visual relationships of personal taste.

In that sense, O'Reilly (2002) argues that taking the task produce with quality, in the professional reality, graphic design is the ruler in our modern empire of images. That is why it the idea that the graphic designer is a simple technician who provides a service reflects a way of thinking unconscious would not be expected from the designers.

Graphic design is the discipline that provides the images and qualities to a culture of consumption design thirsty. Also, product design fuels the desire and consumption, which makes the design, is everywhere, and it is simply the omnipresence of design, what pushes designers to recognize that their work comprises a commercial and social impact.

Since the 60s, graphic design defines and shapes, whether at a public, commercial, corporate or media space. The nature of the work done by the graphic design has changed over the last 4 decades that have passed, as to the business that serves has been internationalized, has taken all the spaces, from the virtual world addressing Internet border to the material appearing multiple design magazines; passing through all the others.

Because contrary to popular belief according Frías (2004) design fulfills the function of plan and create products and services allows achieving a higher standard of living.

Direct from management of Design Bureau Company, González (2004) points out that "Although a company may start as a casual office, it can acquire a formal character and is important to specify the company with a corporate structure. This part is essential to the operation of an office, because generally designers are disordered in administrative and financial aspects. This impact on the operation of the office and the way customers perceive us; if the idea of order and organizations is not transmitted to customers, it is difficult to win major accounts [...] the growth of the firm will from the hand of the customers and working for multinational clients required to have quality designers [...] But to be seen and correctly perceived by customers, not enough to be a professional design, it is important to give the appearance of being. It is essential that customers no longer see ourselves as we do cartoons." Which tells us that is important to manage with a business organization.

Showing that must be managed with a great sense of administration marketing and design.

The firms affiliated to *"Marca la Diferencia"* [Mark the difference] important business design group of Mexico City, highlight on name of Richard Kirwin (2004) "We need the business sense to establish new rules, so that when the design works is done within the context of business and we need the best design; one that fits the communication of the company, to be truly a successful project. Many companies in the world do not consider in designing the vision of the ultimate consumer, only see the product design; do not consider the whole idea."

In such a way it is necessary to make conscious strategic value of design in business.

For Muñoz (2007) director of the design firm X Design, should be used strategies to reach large customers. "I know whereof we have excellent designers in Mexico and the level of the design is marked by the customer communication and the degree of daring on innovation."

Isabel Mariño, President of the *Sociedad Estatal para el Desarrollo del Diseño y la Innovación (DDI)* [State Society for the Development of Design and Innovation] and General Director of Policy for Small and Medium Enterprises in Spain, mentioned in Isern (2003) comments that, "to modify the wrong vision of design in business that far from favoring the companies themselves, limited their business opportunities the administration develops a series of actions and programs to promote and support the incorporation of design to the strategies of companies and especially the of smaller size."

To Telford (2001) important changes in the business environment caused by the Treaties of Free Trade mainly on North America whose trading activity into the US have potentially grown over recent years has generated increased competition that has forced many small business, to seek help from professional experts in design and marketing to help increase their competitiveness, causing them to stop seeing the use of these services as an expense and appreciating them as an investment.

Bruce & Bessant (2002) mentioned by (Guijosa & Frías, 2006) refer to the relationship between marketing and design is through the symbiosis that exists between the designer and what is called "marketing mix," optimizing the work of designers and marketers.

The process of marketing management includes:

a)   The situational analysis and design strategies to achieve the objectives of the organization.

b)   The implementation of these strategies and control of results.

In other words, marketing management organizes and directs the financial resources for the purpose of the sales will exceed the costs and provide the maximum profit.

Kotler & Armstrong (2003) have noted that in their discipline there are four key elements that mixed can optimize business activities of companies; these are the 4 P's of marketing:

a)   The product: is the design object worth his salt on its communication.

b)   The price: is the compensation of its attributes and their meaning.

c)   Promotion: is the strategy focused directly on the consumer.

d)   The place: Are the location and the atmosphere more propitious for distribution and sale.

The interaction of the four 4 P's with the design and administration is very narrow and can be given in different degrees in the various stages of the marketing mix:

a)   Since the generation of the idea for a new product in the design activities.

b)   On the feasibility of marketing to realize it and the market research.

c)   In the internal and external SWOT analysis from the study of the product and the competence.

d)   In strategic planning and product promotion based on their attributes.

Indeed, improvements to the design management process resulting in a business relationship in which companies operate with the security of having a correct knowledge of the design towards environments that according Hil & Jones (2005) are as follows:

a) Internal: Develops all operational processes that interact within the organization. In them a better solution to the design requirements is claimed.

b) External: Develops all competitive processes that generate interaction with the professional environment. There greater participation is established to the market demands.

Thereby projecting the implementation of the design strategy.

With this and for a better appreciation of strategic design in your business, manage the design needs to develop a great intellectual platform, an important market knowledge and extensive management skills to participate effectively in business with strategy, a quality that applies not only on addressing the customer, enter the market or designing a product but also to convert the design into a permanent consumer satisfier.

Basic concept: A company is positioned to succeed if they have access to an endowment of competitively valuable resources that precipitates positively to their environment of mobility (industry) and competitive sector (commercial entity).

Mobilization of resources in the company to gain a competitive advantage. Adapted from: Thompson, Arthur; Strickland, A. J. *Strategic management. Concepts and cases.* USA: Mc Graw Hill, 2004. 398 pp. p. 121.

Project management

A designer is a planner with an aesthetic sense
BRUNO MUNARI
Designer, poet, sculptor, teacher and Italian author, linked to the Futurist
movement

According Satué (1988) design has developed a series of cognitive processes and techniques that have been adapted to the social context. In the professional environment and for the proper performance of a design project were managed under strict disciplinary measures in order to achieve communicative effectiveness, aesthetic consistency and usability in business, that is that are performed around a consistent organization.

For Hil & Jones (2005) by way of adapting the business environment have been adopted processes with organizational functions that reveal that the design is recognizing the process of emergence of the administration to intervene when appropriate, since the actions of entrepreneurship, running a business and to the development of a project.

According to Bruce et al., (1999) from establishing a business organization, design has focused its attention on the design project management process and their effects.

Into the design project management process and in general terms, there are three major aspects:

1.   Finding the appropriate project for company profile:

Specifically, the method a company uses to find the project more appropriate to its mission to develop it according to its business model, the type of customer or consumer profile. This means being specific to target a business sector and be wise in the market segment.

2.   Drafting of the project requirements or "briefing."

This refers to the method that a company uses for the designer to gather the necessary information for each project and perform design work professionally. Using of these design requirements.

3.   Evaluation of the design project:

That is, the method that the company employs to evaluate the design process steadily and to identify whether it was successful or not the result either:

a.   By contrasting of the design requirements against the product obtained.

b.   Through a simple analysis of the costs of the design against the increase in the product sales and permanence in the market.

In this way and in respect any organization, the design project management process should be implemented in:

a.   A design company.

b.   A company with a design department.

c.   A company that hires design services.

In order to harmonize the processes between professional design services, the design department and a company that hires design services, whether micro, small, medium or large, from any industry. Considering that its main aim is to develop as an internal process of the company and create a product or service as efficiently as possible.

In this regard Peter Gorb and Angela Dumas (mentioned by Frías, 2004) teachers from the Open University in England, include the term "silent designers," they refer to those professionals not designers, who take design decisions that affect the development of a design project and in many cases, deteriorates the final result.

Similarly, Cooper (1995) (quoted by Iduarte & Zarza, 2004) indicates that the phenomenon of silence design is recognized because the professional designer is replaced by other people as their own managers or owners of companies and appears to be due, in part, to the existence of "software design" easy to use, or to the close relationship of the owner with the customers who makes them think that knows better than anyone their needs and preferences.

It can also happen when professional designers do not engage fully in the project design and not involved in the decision making of the project leaving it in the hands of untrained people to resolve it correctly.

Telford (2001) comments that are still very few Mexican companies that understand the concepts of professionalism, service and design, ergo, that in general terms the design cost is still perceived as an expense rather than as an investment and there is a marked lack of information from managers on the differential advantages that the proper use of the design can bring to their businesses.

According to Daniels (2000) the most obvious reason for failure of the use of the design is the low ability to have employers to define project requirements.

In this regard, Frías (2004) comments that in the planning of any design task is needed drawing up a list of requirements or "briefing;" this document should contain in general rational design data more information for administrative and marketing aspects, which must be requested and analyzed throughout the interdisciplinary team involved in the development of a design project and to the best extent possible to determine the cost, price and product attributes.

According to the Australian designer Ken Kato (mentioned by Frías 2004) based on the briefing, is generated graphical information needed to make visible the intangible.

By forming an idea in the development of a design project, part of the work to be performed in the design process is to incorporate the emotional benefits for placing a product on the market, these should be reflected in the attributes of its image and shape: its visual impact; therefore is first order to know which involves positioning.

Kotler & Amstrong (2003) warns that the position of a product relates how consumers define the product based on two important attributes:

1.   The place the product occupies in the minds of consumers, in relation to competitor products.

2.   The implementation of the distinctive benefits and brand differentiation in the minds of consumers.

As an example, Sobrino & Mercado (2006) argue that, "in addition to the product, departmental stores and supermarkets are always looking for innovative, ingenious, useful and fun ways to get our attention, its objectives are to increase their sales and the flow of buyers and ensure loyalty of their customers. To achieve this requires a constant effort of research and analysis of the needs and trends of its various markets. On them are of all kinds of services, since they have a global strategy and apply their proven formulas elsewhere, there is also an emotional and psychological strategy and is directed to our feelings and emotions." In this sense the design contributes to all of this.

In this regard Guijosa & Frías (2006) state that, "with the changing trends in consumer behavior observed, especially in the decade of the 90s, with increasingly competitive environments and business orientation directed towards the identification and satisfaction the needs of consumers, both mass consumption goods and called luxury goods, the design has taken on a new role: It has become a strategic tool of marketing. The tangible product attributes are now a clear motive to purchase by their ability to communicate not only rational attributes such as functionality, but a strong, coherent imaginary, recognizable and unique."

They claim that, "design plays a very important role in marketing because the visual impact of design provides the product, makes a big difference between one product and another, achieving ranges of choice, and thus influence the buying behavior of a consumer, this influence has been the product of the new role that globalization and the manifestation of consumption have experienced, so the design contributes to the main objective of the company: profitability, as it provides added values to a product and economic entities that produce it."

Although it is noted that the greatest attribute of design flourishes of conception and begins from its reflection.

According to Isern (2003), "As a discipline, design is not yet sufficiently widespread among enterprises, although there are notable examples of companies that have successfully adopted differentiation strategies based on design, still part of our business community ignores the potential of this tool for innovation and improvement. A little appreciation of the ability of the design to provide benefits and competitive advantages to the corporate initiatives causes that, in many cases, is seen the part of many employers as an expense rather than as an investment."

Now, "the main goal of the design is to contribute to spread the culture of innovation among small and medium enterprises to assimilate design as a key factor in the differentiation and success of its products and services."

"The examples of applications on design and its contribution to the success that has been endorsed by its projection on the market, reflecting the strong commitment of many companies that have opted for to add value to their products and services, differentiate and improve the communication with their customers."

As demonstrated by several investigations in first world countries, as indicated (Jeffrey & Hunt 1985; Bruce et al, 1999; Olson et al, 2000) the professional use of design can positively influence the functioning of the company provided that they are administered effectively.

In this sense, it is of utmost importance to have well identified joint work of the disciplines which impact directly on the definition of the requirements of a design project.

Several authors as (Faust, 2000; Bouchenoire, 2000; and Kalderman, 1991) cited by Iduarte & Zarza (2004) agree that an adequate communication between the employer and the designer is a key element to project success. It is in this course when you have to take into consideration a thorough analysis between administration (mission, vision, strategies, and so on), marketing (needs that must satisfy the new product, market segment to which it is addressed, among others) and design (technical specifications, consumer demands, and so on).

The key that is needed to achieve it is being aware of their relationship and project it judiciously in drafting of the design requirements.

ARTIUX

Basic concept: Every company should use a brief to delineate the characteristics of your design project.

1. PRODUCT CATEGORY:	5.1.1 Primary competition
2. BRAND:	5.1.2 Secondary competition
3. NAME, PRODUCT, AND PRESENTATION:	5.1.3 Generic competition
3.1 Physical overview	5.2 Regional segmentation
3.1.1 Detailed product description	5.2.1 Segmentation by brand
3.1.2 Detailed description of the packaging	5.2.2 Segmentation by presentation
3.1.3 Consumer habits	5.2.3 Segmentation by price
3.1.4 Buying habits	5.3 Overall market participation
3.2 Conceptual emotional product description	5.3.1 Share of market
3.2.1 Basic earnings of product	5.3.2 Share of voice
3.2.2 Evidence supporting the product / consistency, color, smell, special flavor	5.4 Impact dimension
3.2.3 Reason Why / Main reason for your choice	5.4.1 Sales volume
4. TARGET AUDIENCE:	6. MARKETING STRATEGY:
4.1 Demographic Profile / gender, age, occupation, SEL, education level, place of residence	6.1 Price
4.2 Psychographic profile / lifestyle, leisure, social style	6.2 Distribution
4.3 Position of the consumer, of the shopper, of the decider	7. COMMUNICATION STRATEGY:
5. MARKET:	7.1 Target groups
5.1 General competence	7.2 Positioning in the consumer's mind

The Briefing documents. Adapted from: "Brief of Coca-Cola in Argentina, Venezuela and Colombia."
http://es.scribd.com/doc/54536566/Brief-Coca-Cola#scribd

To properly manage your project design is better than your company use the design project management process as a document, which must be filled with their own data. If your company uses for design, a project to another enterprise the document must be filled with data from that company.

116

TEQUILA SUNRISE FOR BUSINESS

Basic concept: Using the design projects management process in a company is the appropriate way to inform, designing and successfully evaluate a product on the market.

1. COMPANY INFORMATION. Based on business process management. (Administration).	
Company:	Values:
Philosophy:	Age:
Mission:	Size (No. of members):
Vission:	Sector of presence: (countries, regions)
2. BRIEF. Define market objectives. (Marketing). Starts the creative process of the project. (Design).	
Product category:	Primary competition
Brand:	Secundary competition
Name, product, and presentation:	Generic competition
Physical overview	Regional segmentation
Detailed product description	Segmentation by brand
Detailed description of the packaging	Segmentation by presentation
Consumer habits	Segmentation by price
Buying habits	Overall market participation
Conceptual emotional product description	Share of market
Basic earnings of product	Share of voice
Evidence supporting the product / consistency, color, smell, special flavor	Impact dimension
Reason Why / Main reason for your choice	Sales volume
Target audience:	Marketing strategy:
Demographic Profile / gender, age, occupation, SEL, education level, place of residence	Price
Psychographic profile / lifestyle, leisure, social style	Distribution
Position of the consumer, of the shopper, of the decider	Communication strategy:
Market:	Target groups
General competence	Positioning in the consumer's mind
Calculation of project implementation	
Campaign objectives	Launch date of the project
Time to develop the campaign	Budget
Deliver to revision for receiving as a corrected brief with comments for its arrangement	
3. EVALUATION. Rate results, set changes, recycle planned and reactive strategies. (Of Management, Marketing, and Design).	
Congruence between product results against all points of the brief and the profile of the company	Increased sales and consumer preference

The design project management process. Adapted from: Bruce et al. (1999) and: http://es.scribd.com/doc/54536566/Brief-Coca-Cola#scribd

Innovation

There are three responses to a piece of design: yes, no and wow! Wow is the one
to aim for
MILTON GLASER
Renowned American graphic designer

According to the RAE (2012), the term innovation means the creation or modification of a product and its introduction in the market.

The Organization for Economic Cooperation and Development [OECD] (2005) in the Oslo Manual distinguishes innovation in four areas: product, process, marketing and organization. Stresses according to data from its first edition in 1992; product innovations and process are well known in the business sector, while marketing innovations and organizational changes are known only by companies in some countries.

The OECD defines innovation as, "the introduction of a new or significantly improved product (good or service), of a process, a new marketing method or a new organizational method in business practices internal, the organization of the workplace or external relations."

The manual suggests that to have innovation, we need at least the product, process, marketing method or method of organization are new or significantly improved for the enterprise; it has been introduced in the market and has been used effectively.

Schumpeter (1978) defines innovation as an invention that is introduced in the market, ie, with potential for industrialization and market.

Ensure that incremental innovations are those that improve a product, service or existing method, but "fall under the static analysis" because it does not explain the social transformations.

For him, what matters are the radical innovations, those original ideas completely new grabbing the entire market and are capable of causing "revolutionary" changes.

Emphasizes that the innovator is not any entrepreneur who rides a business, not a capitalist, nor technical "expertise," this entrepreneur is the person who has the capacity and initiative to propose and implement new combinations of means of production, to wit, the person with no business or business is capable of generating and managing radical innovation within organizations or outside them.

According to De Jong, Vanhaverbeke, Kalvet, & Chesbrough (2008) in the spring of 2003, the book "Open Innovation," was published by Chesbrough who coined this term for the first time. According to Chesbrough, traditionally many companies went through innovation closed most of the twentieth century, with which business projects are managed exclusively with knowledge, internal sources and means of own organization also the materialization economic performance is achieved exclusively through the incorporation of such knowledge into products of their own portfolio.

To Argote & Ingram (2000) under the classical model, companies protect the transfer of knowledge to competitors, projects can only begin within the company and end up in their own market.

Definitely, Chesbrough (in De Jong, et al., 2008) says that protect their knowledge are measures of the past given to increasing presences: personnel highly experienced and qualified, growing presence of private venture capital, faster and faster time to market for many products and services, increased competition from foreign companies due to ongoing globalization and broader knowledge from different sources share, bring as a consequence that companies must open their doors; is widely believed that the era of open innovation has come.

Brant & Lohse (2014) mention that Chesbrough in 2006 defines open innovation as the use of inputs with purpose and outflows of knowledge to accelerate internal innovation while expanding markets for external use. This model involves strategic information exchanges managed with actors outside the boundaries of an organization, which aims is to integrate their resources and knowledge in their own innovation process.

In other words, according to De Jong, et al., (2008) open innovation is a proactive resource used in companies to exit the internal boundaries of their organization and where cooperation with various external professionals have a key role. Means combining internal knowledge with external to take forward the projects with R & D (research & development) for bring to market innovative products. Companies must do enough R & D to be economically dynamic and have the absorptive capacity to conduct a professional dialogue and learn from their external environment.

Under this scenario is possible to classify innovation:

As the OECD (2005) says: By their nature:

1.   Product innovation: that is to introduce to the market new or improved products or services.

2.   Process innovation: as an effect of applying new or improved methods of business in production processes.

3.   Marketing innovation: it derives to open a new market or implement better structures in a market.

4.   Organizational innovation: as a result of creating a new or better way of managing or sources of supply.

Based on Schumpeter (1978): On the degree of originality:

1.   Incremental: when there are only improvements made to a product, service or existing method.

2.   Radical: when there is an original combination, different applications or new concepts in order to obtain a result completely new to hoard the entire market.

According to Chesbrough (in De Jong, et al., 2008): Regarding its emergence:

1.   Closed Innovation: when innovation arises only from one organization to a single niche.

2.   Open innovation: when the innovation is the integration of various organizations towards the world increasingly diversified.

The crucial recommendation is to opt for open innovation and protect their intellectual property through patents, copyrights and trademark.

Under the scene, De Jong, et al., (2008) it can be pointed that the creation, survival, growth and transfer of private knowledge between companies are behaviors that foster the entrepreneurial spirit of people fact that makes define *the discovery* as the evaluation, organization and execution of opportunities when therefrom, entrepreneurs start something new, are persistent and proactive in its realization.

For the OECD (2005) there are two main reasons for using new criteria to the company as a minimum requirement of innovation. First, adopt innovations to innovate in the improvement of goods and second disseminate the initial innovations to other companies that are new to them.

For Porter & Scott (2001), "innovation has become the key challenge for global competitiveness. To manage it well, companies must harness the power of location to create and market new ideas."

To Brant & Lohse (2014) is expected to open innovation will become the model of innovation twenty-first century. Well in fact, having ideas is simple, have good ideas it is more complicated, but it really is a strategic challenge for companies is to continuously generate real good ideas into products and services with commercial success in the market.

Robert Hayes (mentioned by Frías, 2004) Robert Hayes (mentioned by Frías, 2004) stated that in the 60s and 70s companies compete based on price, during the late 70s and early 80s they taught with quality, however predicted that from the late 80s they would with design.

Isern (2003) designer and editor of the *Guía Creativity* magazine in Spain, believes it is necessary that managers of design and the directors of communication of companies disposal of the design as a tool to optimize the professional management, aiming to generate business between companies in different sectors with the will of establishing criteria, enhance synergies between these, open perspectives new markets and stimulate the binomial supply and demand; consequently increase the value of design in a country.

Highlighting to the design is an essential element of innovation.

Basic concept: Competition among firms causes innovate to gain advantages, these are a reflection of leadership approaches that establish a future prognosis way as to extend its dominance in the management, marketing and creativity in large sections.

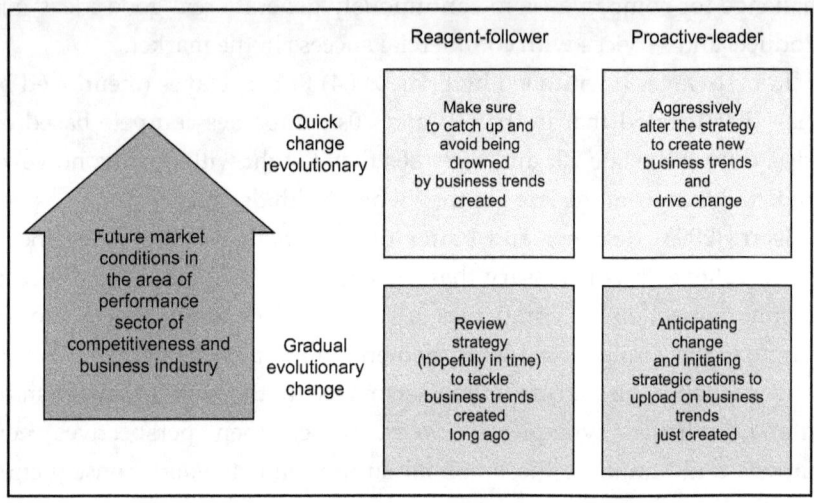

	Reagent-follower	Proactive-leader
Quick change revolutionary	Make sure to catch up and avoid being drowned by business trends created	Aggressively alter the strategy to create new business trends and drive change
Gradual evolutionary change	Review strategy (hopefully in time) to tackle business trends created long ago	Anticipating change and initiating strategic actions to upload on business trends just created

Future market conditions in the area of performance sector of competitiveness and business industry

Strategic approaches to prepare business with a view to future market conditions. Adapted from: Thompson, Arthur; Strickland, A. J. *Strategic management. Concepts and cases*. USA: Mc Graw Hill, 2004. 398 pp. p. 17.

The ice on background | PART 3
Pervading Grenadine

You need the kind of objectivity that makes you forget everything you've heard,
clear the table, and do a factual study like a scientist would
STEVE WOZNIAK
American inventor, engineer, computer programmer and entrepreneur

MARÍA ASUNCIÓN ARAMBURUZAVALA
Founder of Tresalia Capital, shareholder and director of AB-InBev

Take the reins.

"I have never seen myself in terms of money, power, I am a normal woman. The first thing on the list of importance to me is my family. I wake up every day thinking about the people I love, what I'm going to do in the office, creating better companies, bringing prosperity to Mexico, bringing employment. That is who I really am. The other, I do not see myself in those terms.

I believe that there are two types of wealth, internal wealth, which is when you feel calm with yourself and satisfied with what you really do and how you do it. And, on the other hand, I think there is the wealth that is money. And for me wealth in money is simply a unit of measurement. It is the way in which you measure the success that you are achieving when undertaking.

[...] Generally the process is, we are always actively looking for new businesses, so my people are dedicated to looking for those new businesses, or, many times, I even have my ideas of things that I read, of things that inspire you, and then we start with a process to try to understand first, what the industry is about, what is the context of that industry, what is around it, then, what is the dynamics of the business and how it competes with other people, and, the truth is that in that process, let's say, of research, of obtaining data, of understanding, one begins to feel ... it is something that I cannot explain exactly ... but one begins to have a feeling that this is something that can be. Then, when one finishes that process, because the numbers confirm it or do not confirm it, but it does end up being already as experience, sensitivity, many years of seeing many things.

[...] My strength is my high conviction, I do not do things that I am not completely, internally convinced and I have a lot of discipline and a lot of seriousness in things, and I think that is what really at the end of the day, that discipline, that constant effort It has taken me to places where I have been able to do things.

[...] My weakness is impatience; I like to see results quickly. I am totally results-oriented, not that I don't have a long term, but I like that actions bring results.

[...] As a leader, always at the front. I like to take the reins of the horse, but when things get difficult, I am not the type to be scared and hide. I am not behind the skirt of my people. I always take responsibility for my things. And when things are going well, we share success and pride. And when things go wrong, we share those bad times, but I'm always in front and I don't like to put people in front.

[...] In my trusted team, at the beginning, when my dad really died, the great support we had was obtained from Joaquín Sordo Barba. After that, I had a person who had been doing business with me for many years, it was my right hand, which is this Juan Pablo Andrade. Now, obviously it's Rodrigo Besoy, in the Tresalia part. I have in 'Privé educatie' Eduardo Holschneider. I have in all the technology part my partner Sergio Rosenhouse and Antonio Rayo. And obviously in 'Real State' Guillermo Vulcano. Each and every one of them is unquestionably much better than me, and, I think that it has been a little really luck and success that we have because really all my people are worth a lot.

[...] The person that I have really always admired and who has always been like the person who has made me the person I am, is my mom. Maybe it's a bit of a hackneyed answer, but that's what I feel deep down inside. My mom seems to me to have been a completely exemplary woman. Through what she taught us, she was the one who forged me and gave me the characteristics that make me today the woman I am.

[…] You always have your "wish-list" that is being renewed in life, and if not, life would not have a joke because you would not want to live, or at least you would be missing that little jacket; At work, in business, I always have a new project, something I want to develop, an idea, or simply from the companies that we have, how to make them grow, how to make them stronger, how to take away risk, there is always something.

[…] The future that awaits us is a very different future than we could imagine, for example, artificial intelligence, the part of digital printing, robotics is going to be very important, the part of technology is also very important. There are many edges, but basically those things I think have the potential to truly change the way business is done and are going to effectively destroy many companies that today we think are indestructible. And I think that is something that many CEOs already understand, and that they are already thinking in what ways that disruption can come and how the company will also adapt to that disruption. We also hope to participate in all this change.

[…] I have several hobbies, the truth is that I really like cycling, I read a lot of business because that is my theme, technology of that kind of thing." (Aramburuzavala, 2016)

LARRY ELLISON
Founder & CEO of Oracle Corporation

Win with love.

"I'd think we have two fundamental drives in our life, we want to be loved; you want to pleased people. And we know a think we know a reason. And these are often quite ons. Because the rest to believe in certain things are correct, you know, we have to work, we are here a certain length, dress a certain way, and if you want to be loved, you want to be accepted by your peers, you want to be accepted by your family, it's an intention earned, and sometimes we're pleasing our parents, sometimes we're pleasing our peers.

But often, just conforming to some fashion, picking out what the group wants from us, and then, conforming to that, because we want to be accepting and love. But there is other fundamental drive inside of us, their work is offer tension between the two, and that is the body think, the body reason; the body come to conclusions, what works and what doesn't, what's fair and what's not fair, what's right and what's wrong. And when fashion and pursuit of love, gets in conflict with the reason, too often, fashion on pursuit of love, wins. In my case didn't.

[...] Think things of yourself, come to adjustments, it's don't simply conform to conventional ways of thinking, conventional ways addressing, conventional ways of acting, but a lot of this. A lot of things are based on fashion, even morality a times is based on fashion. It was one side. Slavery was once not considered, not to be immoral, you know, people are shocked to that.

The ancient Greeks had slaves, that did had slavery in this country as recently as a thirty or forty years ago, so there are more of that, you have to really go back to first principles, and think things out for yourself, with the scientific principles, or moral principles, or business ideas, or product ideas, you have to think things of yourself.

The opportunity in this country is astounding; everyone who works hard and be able cleverly, has the opportunity, you know, to make almost anything possible.

And not see the American dream, anything here is possible, we are not hold back that immigrants come here, and in a single generation do extraordinary things, this country is not perfect, but compared with every other country in the world, is absolutely fabulous and there's unlimited opportunity, it requires hard work, requires little very luck, but still in America anything is possible." (Ellison, 2013)

HOWARD SCHULTZ
Chairman and CEO of the Starbucks Coffee Company

I am because of you, be because of me.

"Thank you, President Crow, for that generous introduction. I really appreciate our friendship and everything we're doing together. Thank you to the Arizona Board of Regents, faculty, and special guests. Congratulations to the graduating class of 2017. And those who are here to support you on this very very special day. And to our 330 Starbucks College Achievement Plan graduate, who have benefitted from the Starbucks and ASU partnership. I am incredible proud to be your partner. Congratulations to all of you.

I would like to begin my time with you today by sharing a personal story. Last year Starbucks Coffee Company opened our first store in South Africa in Johannesburg. I had never been in South Africa before, did not know what to expect. Certainly, could not be prepared for the level of poverty and what I saw in the townships throughout the city. We opened two stores and lines were out the door in anticipation of Starbucks coming to the market. But before we opened the stores, I gathered the 50 young people who would grace the green apron and put on the Starbucks apron and represent the company. I sat with them for a few hours and wanted to hear each one of their personal stories. And as they were sharing their stories with me, despite their poverty, their plight in life, there was so much joy and gratitude in their hearts. But what I learned was two things.

One, all of 50 of these young people had never had a job before. They were all unemployed for their entire life. And you should see the self-esteem and the sense of security as they were getting ready for their first job. But the second lesson was as they were going around the room and talking to me about their story, I kept hearing an African word I had never heard before. A word that Nelson Mandela used all the time. The word is "ubuntu" and finally, I got up the courage and I asked, "What does this word mean that you keep using?" And they couldn't wait to share it with me. And in unison, they said, "Howard, ubuntu means I am because of you."

As I have the honor to speak with you today, I ask you to keep that story in mind, because everything I'm going to share with you today is through the lens of ubuntu. I grow up in Brooklyn, New York, in public housing, the projects, as it was called back then. My parents were both high school drop-outs, and they could barely afford $96 dollars a month rent in our two-bedroom apartment for my brother, my sister, and my parents. However, from my earliest of memories, my mother instilled in me her belief in the American dream and the promise of America: that a good education and hard work will open the doors to a better life. And that provides me with an important lesson to share with you all today. That your station in life does not define you and the promise of America that is for all of us.

When I was seven years old, I had a defining moment in my life, I came home from school one day and saw my father laid on a couch with a cast from his hip to his ankle. He had a series of terrible blue-collar jobs as a high school drop-out, army bet, but this particular job he had in 1960 was probably the worst. He was a truck driver delivering and picking up cloth diapers before the invention of Pampers. He fell on a sheet of ice in March of 1960. And in March of 1960, if you were a blue-collar uneducated worker, you were dismissed if you had an accident. No workman's compensation, no severance, and no health insurance. And I saw the fracturing of the American dream and I saw my parents go through hopelessness and despair at the age of seven. And those scars, that shame, that is with me even today. As a young boy, I could have never imagined that I would one day build a company of my own.

Let alone, a company that would have more than 26,000 stores in 75 countries and employ more than 300,000 people. But from day one, I really wanted to build the kind of company my father never got a chance to work for. A company that honors and respects the dignity of work and the dignity of all men and all women. And that is why became the first company in all of America to provide comprehensive health insurance 30 years ahead of the Affordable Care Act, as well as ownership in the form of stock options for all of our employees, including part-time people. Because it is my firm belief, that success in business and in life is best when it's shared. Starbucks Coffee Company went public in 1992, and from 1992 to 2006, we were on a magical carpet ride in which everything we did turned to gold. But in 2007, the music stopped. We have lost sight of our shared purpose and our guiding principles in which grow and success began to cover up mistakes and a disease set in to Starbucks. That disease? Hubris. We lost our way, and believe it or not, we almost lost the entire company. During this cataclysmic period, I was reminded what it means to love something and the responsibility that goes with it, as well as an understanding that leadership and moral courage is not a passive act. My parents and I took it personally and we transformed the entire company. We galvanized the entire organization around our core values and servant leadership. Every business, every organization, even every family must to be true to its values and reason for being. Our core purpose and reason for being then and now has always been to achieve the fragile balance between profit and humanity. Today the equity of Starbucks brand has never been stronger, and our track record of creating shareholder value and social impact over the last 25 years has virtually been unparalleled. We have built one of the most respected and recognized brand in the world, with the view that today the rules of engagement for business and business leaders have changed, that we must do more for our people and the communities we serve.

And most importantly, that not every business decision is an economic one, and that success is not an entitlement. It has to be earned and earned every day through the lens of humility. Only in America can a poor kid from a public housing have the privilege and the honor to be the commencement speaker at the largest and most innovative university in the country. I stand before you as living proof of the American dream joining many of your parents, your professors, and generations of graduates before you, but today you may question the strength of that dream and the promise of America. That's fair. My generation has not made it easy for you. Our political leaders on both sides of the aisle have not acted with enough courage, nor honesty, in addressing the long-term challenges we face. They have been more focused and fighting with each other than walking in the shoes of the American people. And vitriol and self-interest rule the day in Washington. Despite of that, when I look to the future, I am extremely optimistic, especially when I look out and see you, because the future is not up to them, not up to Washington, it's up to you. This milestone in your life may come with some anxiety about what tomorrow holds and you may have questions that only time can answer, but as a young man who once sat nervously at this own commencement, I encourage you to always trust yourself and to be mindful of these three enduring questions: How will you respect your parents and honor your family? How will you share your success and serve others with dignity? And, how will you lead with humility and demonstrate moral courage?

You're leaving this campus as the best-prepared generation in the history of our country. You each possess entrepreneurial spirit, the passion, and the commitment to create the future you deserve. However, don't stop there. Try not to rely only on what you have learned in the classroom. Summon your compassion, your curiosity, your empathy to others, and your commitment to service. Give more than you receive, and I promise you, it will come back to you in ways you can't possibly imagine. Each of you are here today because of someone else, a parent, a sibling, a teacher, a neighbor, a mentor, someone who had faith and confidence in you like my mother had in me and nurtured your dreams. As you leave here today take a moment to think of those who have come before you, who have helped you along the way, who are at your side today. If they are here, embrace them and thank them for the gift of education and the support and the love that day have given you.

Your generation can bring people together like no other. You can innovate, create, and lead. Your generation will transform our economy and create millions of new jobs. You will develop cleaner energy. You will make it so racism only exists in history books. Yes, you will. You will be the generation that teaches the world that we are at our best when we recognize respect, and celebrate our diversity. You can, and you will make your mark on our country and our shared humanity. Dream big and then dream bigger. A more innovative dream. A more inclusive dream. All of you will preserve and enhance the promise of America, the promise that propelled me out of public housing, the promise that will propel you forward, regardless of the color of your skin, your religion, your gender, your sexual orientation, or you station in life. Please remember that. ASU is because of you. You are because of ASU. We are because of each other. Ubuntu! Yes, say it with me: Ubuntu! Go forward and continue to make your parents and your family proud. God bless you and thank you and congratulations to the class of 2017. Thank you." (Schultz, 2017)

Tasting the perfect combination
The Tequila Sunrise about to ice

When you go for something, don't come back until you get it
WILLIAM CLEMENT STONE
American businessman, philanthropist and self-help books author

The relevance of these three ingredients come from have understood them as a triune energy. I mean the original energy that exists everywhere and whatever it is to project success. This is because it always seeks three objectives: to generate order, to achieve expansion and to leave evidence. It is the way it operates. In business it exists by representing order with management, expansion with marketing and evidence with design. And if you are thinking about business, it will be arranged to properly activate as tripartite energy and achieve its mission in business. It works under a truth. The triune unit. The one that leaves us at all times and everywhere a trace, that we follow by instinct of compatibility of our natural being with its natural origin and that trail allows us to find the spark that reaffirms its presence and leads us to realize how to cross the path that leads to success, because we always seek to prosper and she seek will manifest. To project them here as business disciplines.

In short, it is about managing the power of Triune Energy in a tripartite way in business, which reveals the mastery that we must develop in order to start up every business process.

The fact of triumphing in life is thanks to that unique tripartite energy that the universe gives to everything that exists. That energy is expressed and reacted effectively in nature. And when activated correctly and in unison in anything with a well-defined objective, consequently it is successfully achieved. Even in any projection that is generated from an idea. Only that in this case when it is misunderstood, omitted or ignored some of its forces, consequently its frequency is not generated and the energy will not work properly.

Whenever energy was expressed in our society from the natural reality was used to insert it as the commercial system and manage its strength to create the artificial reality in which we live, despite this from the artificiality it is possible for everyone to realize how really works the universe with a perfect system of creation and natural patterns that are everywhere and are the ones that communicate to us the way to establish connection with the universal nature, the form is to enter into it, to notice the flow of the energy of the universe and its three forces to finally be activated in order to create as a better reality and leave the false system that surrounds us.

To recover the correct direction carries the force of triune energy, which naturally moves life and establish it again in the means of survival of the present society, we must be guided by a process.

First, we must know in general how to develop the triune energy in business, the three main disciplines that make success. Once understanding how it has been successful to raise organizations that today are conceived as companies, how has managed to move large masses of people to what is now called the market and how it has achieved to captivate millions of people which are commonly referred to as consumers. Then it will be important to know thoroughly all the full development of the Tequila Sunrise to understand how it works in every person and have the necessary fundamentals that determine control the process of manifestation of reality both in your life and in your business.

This process occurs always at the quantum scale, that is, at high speed and in tiny. And to maintain it, it increases its strength in what we call time and space. So, let's continue to learn it in business.

Whenever your company generates a visualization it is because it has originated an observation from its administration where it begins to concentrate the energy with strategic thinking which represents the strength of tequila energy and responds to its business plan by projecting a particle impregnated with that intention as an initial probability that runs through its entire structure, so that when passing to the department of marketing leaves there the tendency of that instruction to concentrate the energy with competitive feeling which represents the malleability of the energy of the orange that requires to manifest with the market study so that it can be formed as memory, so it is expected to have the complete instruction sending the particle with the results to the design department complementing in response to that instruction with the corresponding innovative emotion, That represents the sweetness of the energy of the grenadine where through the use of the brief creates a good product to be able to turn it into an intense experience.

So that particle full of strategic thinking and innovative emotion in agreement, rise again to marketing with the accumulated instruction where the contents are generated that complete the required competitive feeling. And combined with the right dose as thought, emotion and feeling, spread the campaign to reach the highest penetration and coverage leaving indelible that observation in the memory of the target market lived as an experience, according to the strength of intention with a view to constantly surpassing the limits that the organization has reached.

Taking effect on consumer appeal who when observing your product memorizes it, and experiencing its benefits by interaction and purchase, feels increasingly safety getting to follow you. What causes back the experienced effect when collaborating on interaction, making following the same effect that gives them back, as the construction of Sunrise, their deepest needs for command (when projecting the character that reflects your management), convincing (when projecting the love that reflects your marketing), and transformation (when projecting the attitude that reflects your design), that gives them security for their interaction. Which means they are sharing the Sunrise Effect you put in their minds. Returning to you the magnetism of what you do.

When this process happens, it is because it has been thoroughly observed and taken to action, it is thus a vibration of joy in the company is caused because it is understood how a controlled state of constant success arises and is due to has activated the triune energy of the universe within the business.

That is, the energetic power of Tequila has been activated, which is the first foundation that generates order and structure, which in business is the administration with which a company is invigorated by giving it the tools that will give it a strong presence. Projecting Character.

At the same time, it has activated the bittersweet power of Orange, which is the second foundation that generates malleability and expansion, which in business is the marketing with which a company is tempered by providing it with the tools that will give it flexible diffusion. Spreading Love.

And it has also activated the sweet power of the Grenadine, which is the third foundation that generates forceful and evidence conviction that in business is the design with which a company is controlled by endowing it with tools that will give it attraction and convincement. Provoking Attitude.

Action that causes to concentrate a great accumulation of energy with three complementary frequencies to magnetize to itself like a single energy (your well-matched businesses in action), which literally begins to open a vortex of energy (your correct use of business plan, market study and design brief), which begins to attract what you want for your company (effective implementation of the SWOT, 4 p's, and LESI), sharing the last result of your materialization (your product), to manifest what you want from when you want it (Launch), consistently attracting energy particles that require the same compatibility Your consumer) and raise in them the combined materializing their reality (obtaining the Sunrise) getting their energy support as a result of your cocktail (you get the Sunrise) materializing your reality in business.

If you want to succeed in your business starts visualizing the panorama of the Sunrise Effect that you want, so that through your best intention impregnated with the energy of the three ingredients, provoke greatness in the business you really want. This process will develop better character, love and attitude that will leave an indelible mark that will distinguish to your business. Take care of all the details because you will develop the seal that characterizes you as your firm, and that will materialize in your business.

In such a manner it is extremely important to emphasize that as part of the business process, this proposal demonstrates that:

1.   To satisfy the buyer must make proper use of the briefing, and it is important to have a strong knowledge of design project management process, to achieve empower them with the attitude demanding and want to experience; through design.

Which requires that:

2.   To understand the consumer must do a good market research, and it is indisputable have a strong knowledge of marketing

management process, in order to address them with the love they need and want to keep; through marketing.

And in turn requires that:

3. To lead the target audience must project a strong business plan, and it is undeniable have a strong knowledge of strategic management process, for their loyalty with the character that guides them and to which feel they belong; through administration.

Which left uncovered that in every business process and for its proper functioning, development of management, marketing, and design is necessary, as the three disciplines which pose the arguments to win in business, because working together can achieve a correct performance and optimum projection at the highest level of business, if treated properly. As suggested by the study by Artiux (2016). Which means that, the administration is projected on the business plan to be *comprised* as the *character* of the company that provides presence and *confidence* to the audience through their *corporate image*, which it is *constructed* as reference for its *observation*. Marketing is projected on market research, to be *compassionate* with the target audience forming the *love* that gives malleability and *security* to the company and its target market through the *brand*, which is shared to remain in his *memory*. And the design is projected in the briefing, to be *transformed* as the *attitude* that provides satisfaction and *certainty* that demands the consumer to the enterprise through *product design*, which is turned into what saved as their *experience*.

So retaking from the background the importance of studies mentioned, which serve to address their evidence as pieces to enable and ensuring the genuine differential force that detonates win in business, and regarding its relationship with the development of the Tequila Sunrise for Business; is laudable define its nature familiar with the present proposal, which exists in:

1. Increasing interest in design and incorporate it as business process to their businesses by part of small business owners order for the great interest and commitment that entrepreneurs show to the design to be one of the main reasons for the success of design in these types of companies, as indicated by the study of Bruce, Cooper, & Vazquez (1999). That therefore will activate all functions that are related to the design project management process, they shall obtain marketing results and

improve the effects of its business plan to make work a business correctly.

2.   Increase knowledge into the designers on how the Micro, Small, and Medium Enterprises manage and leverage the design, knowing the commitment and understanding of design by managers in order to each design project to be performed in a professional manner, as mentioned by the study of Iduarte & Zarza (2004). Approaching and offering their professional design services, thereby encouraging micro, small, and medium entrepreneurs know the true value of design, be made aware of the commercial impact that can generate investment in design, and adopt it as a process within their companies. This will cause the design be incorporated correctly, a marketing plan be activated, and administration completes its work.

3.   Bear in mind how it is conceived the design, that is, the set of tangible attributes of a product which they are related to a sense of belonging and self-satisfaction, since affect the choice of an individual at the moment making the purchase, because their preferences lean for aesthetic characteristics and its variable need is defined by quality; as well as with what they relates the reasons that consumers have in mind at the moment of purchase, and it is with a value-priced reasoning, based on subjective aspects, that is, with a symbolic added value of emotional affective nature, through the stimuli, feelings, and symbolisms that communicates design, as suggested by the study of Guijosa & Frías (2006). Which together are the elements that must be taken into account in the market study and direct hand from the sample representing the final consumer, to have elements that allow us to conceive a good briefing and design of a product.

4.   Leverage the new mental model that the consumer is now proposing that allows the identification the emotional benefits that promote and influence consumption habits, and these stem from deep needs for reinvention, dominion, security, and connection, which argues the study of Saatchi & Saatchi X mentioned by Lecinski (2011). Because nowadays, buyers want to explore to get the information they need, analyze how products can improve their quality of life, and they are motivated to the global interaction 24/7 with other people to strengthen their relationships while obtaining information. Boosted by the desire to take responsibility for their own identity and well-being of their families

and homes. Creating the crucial Zero Moment of Truth (ZMOT), in which customers will take the first impression of a product and quite possibly they make the final decision, allowing win in the day to day, and will affect the success or failure of almost all brands in the world. Since it is directly related to the correct data collection of a market study in real time and thus, its proper translation at the briefing for the realization of a design project, to project a better product, and affects largely to take effect in the minds of consumers and in generate the decision at the time of purchase.

In all this, jump to light that the Tequila Sunrise for Business has its effect here, when it rises and dawns on the mind of the consumer, as a strategy that ensures a differential force to achieve your goals, gain what you want to achieve and achieve success in your business.

Thus, it is that power of tequila projects the energetic character of the structure of your company, the harmony of orange juice reflects bittersweet love of its malleability in the market, and the forcefulness of grenadine triggers the sweet attitude of their results in the consumer.

Basic concept: The main disciplines of an organization well used shaping the success of the company and maintain the same common goal to create competitive advantages in business strategy.

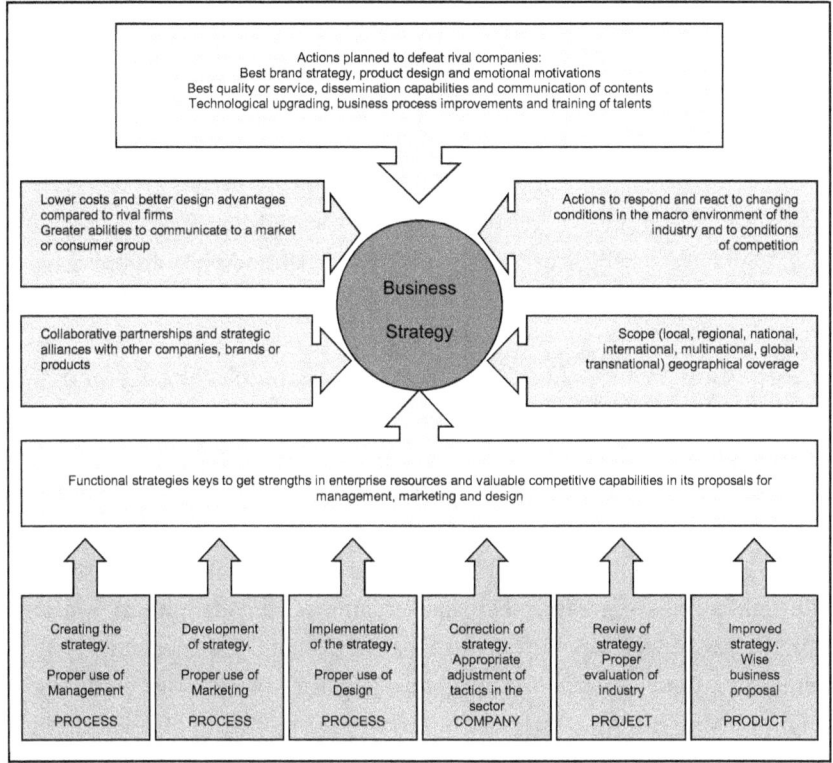

Actions planned to defeat rival companies:
Best brand strategy, product design and emotional motivations
Best quality or service, dissemination capabilities and communication of contents
Technological upgrading, business process improvements and training of talents

Lower costs and better design advantages compared to rival firms
Greater abilities to communicate to a market or consumer group

Actions to respond and react to changing conditions in the macro environment of the industry and to conditions of competition

Business Strategy

Collaborative partnerships and strategic alliances with other companies, brands or products

Scope (local, regional, national, international, multinational, global, transnational) geographical coverage

Functional strategies keys to get strengths in enterprise resources and valuable competitive capabilities in its proposals for management, marketing and design

| Creating the strategy.

Proper use of Management

PROCESS | Development of strategy.

Proper use of Marketing

PROCESS | Implementation of the strategy.

Proper use of Design

PROCESS | Correction of strategy.
Appropriate adjustment of tactics in the sector
COMPANY | Review of strategy.
Proper evaluation of industry

PROJECT | Improved strategy.
Wise business proposal

PRODUCT |

Efforts to create a competitive advantage. Adapted from: Thompson, Arthur; Strickland, A. J. *Strategic management. Concepts and cases.* USA: Mc Graw Hill, 2004. 398 pp. p. 56.

When sunrise at business
Getting the Sunrise Effect

*I want to spend 100 percent of my time focused on what I think I can make the
biggest difference*
MEG WITHMAN
American business executive, political activist, and philanthropist

According Fuentes (2013) the responsible for elevate a brand must
fulfill the mission to better reach the consumer's mind to bill more than
the competition. Reflection that simplifies Don Draper, the fictional
character of the New York advertising agency Sterling Cooper in the
television series Mad Men, who rescues the phrase: "Mine is selling hand
cream ladies. Smoke firefighters take care." An argument inspired by
true geniuses like Draper Daniels, creator of the campaign Marlboro
Man; or Rosser Reeves, impeller of name Colgate. He mentions that the
formula of these precursors of advertising and marketing, converge on
the famous mixture of the four P's (Price, Product, Promotion and Place),
elements combined rationally provide solidity and permanence to a
brand.

Lecinski (2011) as vice president of sales for Google in the US
describes the emergence of the new marketing approach. Mention was
A.G. Lafley from Procter & Gamble who called the 'First moment of
truth' (FMOT), the importance of the seven seconds that elapse between a
buyer is in front of a shelf full, look at the options, and decide which one
to buy. The 'Second Moment of Truth' (SMOT), is when buyer re-buy
convinced that meets its expectations. But there is another, which is prior
and works before the buyer get to the store, is the 'Zero Moment of
Truth' (ZMOT). This new decisive phase was incorporated into the
classic three-step process: stimulus, shelf, and experience. Since buyers
share with each other the information they have obtained on products, in

their own way and at their own pace, passing from the message to the interaction.

According to Cohen (2013) president of Riverside Marketing Strategies, each organization must understand and deal with each of the moments of truth to build and maintain relationships with both existing and potential customers, in order to provide useful content marketing and social media participation.

Framing the three mentioned Moments of Truth and highlights the points where you have to pay attention to be more effective:

Prior to any moment of truth takes initial relevance Stimulus, which includes both the critical instant that projects the released content, such as the indispensable product that promises the emotional attributes which is designed to rise to a need. And climbing does happen one by one the moments of truth.

1.   Zero Moments Of Truth (ZMOT, coined by Google): This is when prospectus recognizes a need and goes online to gather information regarding a potential purchase which is applies to acquiring a wide range of goods and services, including face-to-face meetings.

In that content marketing is necessary. Jay Baer marketing speaker and author calls this 'self-serve information' since where prospectus seeks and use it on their own. Among the options are:
*   Blog posts answering customer questions.
*   YouTube videos showing how to use your product.
*   Pinterest and Instagram images.
*   Slideshare presentations.

Social media engagement: While it's difficult to project when a specific prospectus is at this moment of truth, must leverage the power of your social media presence across venues to provide product information and answer questions.

2.   First Moment Of Truth (FMOT, coined by P&G): When faced with the real product and its related alternatives. On the shelf behavior is considered to be the decision point to buy a brand or specific product.

In that content marketing is necessary. Understand that at this point, your prospectus is more than halfway to making purchasing decisions. Where you should attend:
*   Offer specific products, including product availability, pricing, and shipping information.

- Provide opinions, ratings, customer stories and testimonials.

Social media engagement: In this phase customers come to buy; they are looking for answers to specific questions. If you don't supply them, others in their network including your competitors, will. Among the key social media options are Facebook and Twitter. Ensure you have sales and/or customer service representatives present. Also include your physical address, phone number and email contact on your social media profiles.

3.   Second Moment Of Truth (SMOT, coined by P&G): happens after the customer has bought and started using your brand or product. The resulting experience should support your pre-purchase promises, helping to build a relationship with your audience. The challenge for many businessmen is that they stop providing post-sales content marketing formats. By doing this, they lose out on the potential to convert a one-time customer into a fan.

In that content marketing is necessary. Provide targeted information that helps customers use your products or helps to return them or fix them. Think in terms of showing customers how to use your products.

- Distribute how-to videos and user guides.
- Offer patterns and recipes where appropriate.
- Provide or participate in user forums to support customers.

Social media engagement: Be available to answer customer questions.

Cohen mentions that there is another moment:

4.   Third Moment Of Truth (TMOT, adds that was coined by Pete Blackshaw ex P&G): This happens post-product use. It's when your customer becomes a true fan and he forms opinions that will returns to your brand with new content: word of mouth, ratings, and reviews. At this point, the customer has become a walking endorsement for your business. To ensure that this third moment of truth works for your organization, you must be willing to nudge your customers to act by encouraging them to return to your website, social media profile or other rating site to comment and contribute collateral content. Further, while you can't erase negative comments because you don't like them, you must respond to them and change your behavior.

In that content marketing is necessary. This are targeted communications post-purchase. Use this opportunity to ensure that customers are happy with your product.

Social media engagement: This involves a combination of customer ratings and reviews as well as sharing their product related experiences via a variety of platforms including Facebook, Twitter, Instagram, Pinterest and YouTube. It also includes platforms that aren't always considered social media such as Amazon (the Granddaddy of ratings and reviews), Yelp and TripAdvisor.

In this sense, getting the most out of the three classic ingredients the Tequila Sunrise for Business and all its elements, you should focus completely its great potential on buyer, inviting them to soak up the Sunrise from the Stimulus for your refined coherence of content in social media achieve that sometime within the ZMOT rise of Sunrise Effect in his mind is achieved, realizing that a product carries all the differential characteristics he wants to assume to live them and share, and so from there on prevail and during every moment of truth.

Just thus, the correct combination of the Tequila Sunrise for Business will cause:

1.   Full alignment of the objectives of the company:

That will be reflected in the design of your product, where it is important to understand the Stimulus as an instant, which is trigger initial and necessary to work the MOT when your product is presented, and which creates promises in the mind of the prospectus whoever takes as a reference and he wish to consult; since it is through receive the Stimulus that you can understand when the objectives of the company begin to project compliance to the needs you want to satisfy the consumer, therefore the Stimulus itself, is the instant you present and the way disclosed your product to appear and remain as long as possible in their mind and strengthen in the MOT. Product design and audiovisual contents that conform it, they are largely those who maintain that commitment in all the MOT.

2.   A solidly built and well-articulated project:

Conformed from the market study, translated by the brief to its purpose and project level, and based on the opinions containing consumer demands. Which must be strengthened through product design, the raison d'être of the brand, and tone of communication of audiovisual content to the consumer. A way to develop a consistent atmosphere between product attributes and the needs that the prospectus wants to satisfy, to rise these attributes emotionally in his mind accompanying in each of the moments of truth.

3.   A suitable product with shared qualities:

That convinces by its attributes as well as compliance with its central promise, where reality that projects the product is the perception of the prospectus about what he expects to increase their quality of life. Result of a proper direction of the product to meet face to face with the target audience towards making purchasing decision, with the intention of turning it into consumer and the premise of achieving be the only thing that seeks to obtain at all moments of truth: a product with true character, that generates feelings of brand value, and increase your emotional bond, so that the carrying assume their qualities as their own.

In this way, is that you can see the big picture that the Tequila Sunrise for Business pose, and thus converge their correct use towards the critical moments of truth, based on its effect.

It is from launch, when the stimulus (S) is generated, from where it begins to take effect the outcome of Sunrise, which tries to understand the initial moment in that go up and down the valuable attributes of a brand in the mind of the prospectus, causing submerge to consult in the sphere of ZMOT, to achieve make it your consumer against competition (FMOT), looking to get a satisfactory experience (SMOT), and also turn it into a real fan (TMOT); to when use it, make it back on the other side of the sphere of SMOT, getting again enjoy shopping in the FMOT, and with Sunrise up freely endorsing now from the ZMOT.

In other words, how should prepare Sunrise is to be present inside the mind of a prospectus from the time of stimulus, during all interaction, and especially when they want to establish it, so they can become and convert more people in an avid consumer. The best brands are winning in those crucial moments of truth.

A misapplication of the Tequila Sunrise for Business, determine a poor outcome of the project and will not cause the effect required to win at all moments of truth. The Tequila Sunrise for Business well combined will achieve in the brand and the product Sunrise Effect to operate in all moments of truth. Therefore, a good result of the project as each of the moments of truth, they will support each other.

A brand or product is the material reference and every moment is a sphere of reality to which enters each prospectus or consumer to find the deep needs to assume: the command of his life with the character, the conviction of his actions through the love, and transforming his reality with the attitude that seeks, until a brand grants them in a given product and a faithful content through the right combination, causing the proper effect that sees up in his mind, to select it and extend it to social media.

Sunrise Effect begins when addressing the Stimulus and remains at every Moment Of Truth, and is achieved when it rises in the ZMOT in the consumer's mind.

Basic concept: It's a system to should be efficient throughout the effect that accompanies to the moments of truth, which together make winning to the top brands.

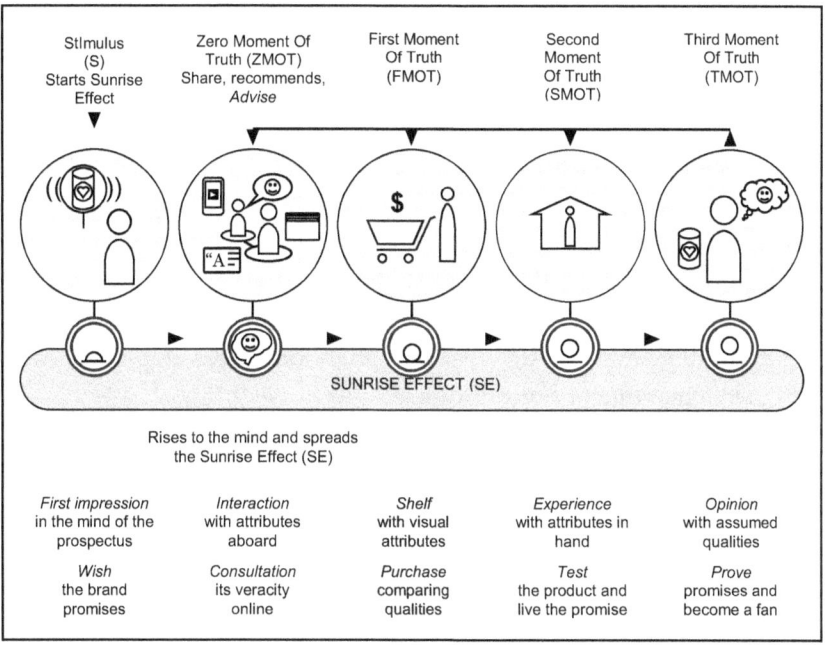

The mental model of purchase. Adapted from: Lecinski, Jim. *Winning the Zero Moment Of Truth.* Illinois: Google Inc., 2011. pp. 16-17. And: http://heidicohen.com/marketing-the-4-moments-of-truth-chart/#sthash.qaOHhTYb.dpuf

Achieve your experience Tequila Sunrise for Business
Let the fiesta begin

Don't limit yourself. You can go as far as your mind lets you. What you believe, remember, you can achieve
MARY KAY ASH
American businesswoman

The recommendation to jump-start the main ingredients and get the experience of the Tequila Sunrise for Business, either as start up or company running, it is to develop the disciplines that support it from the base, is about generating a complete renovation.

The preparation of this cocktail requires living up that needs the strong position of the company, the rapidly changing market, and new consumer demands. To do this, pay attention to develop their classic ingredients that must be carefully selected:

1. The tumbler:

Let's start by making it clear that to achieve the business you imagine; you first need to have a place from where you will develop the processes that govern the ideology of your business. That place should reflect the solidity with which you plant yourself in a sector and the security with which you extend yourself to the world.

The tumbler is the container for your entire "professional business structure;" it is the material and intellectual capital, that is, your physical facilities and your most select personnel with which you will achieve all your movements and achieve what you want to reach. And as a support where you must pour the ingredients to develop its best aspects, it needs to have some broad and unique qualities to receive the combination, contain the correct dose, and share its effect inside and outside it; it must be large enough in order to be prepared for all the activities it will generate inside and be specially distributed to contain a correct workflow. Therefore, get ready with the right tumbler that is the body of your business where your capital will put your "business plan" into action.

Your tumbler is the physical structure of your company that has a presence from its location and represents your company wherever you appear, it must be adequate, portentous and transparently visible.

2.   Ice cubes:

So, we come to the ice, which is the business intention of wanting to win and make win, which you direct to the consumer. Intention that arises from the high command and grows in its journey as it characteristically shapes the skills you have in each ingredient. At every moment that you carry out your corresponding activities, you collaborate with making that intention work, which is shared among the entire team through the line of intellectual production flow and that forms a uniform cluster of particles that blend together as part of the cocktail cool the mixture until you reach the material realization.

Ice has long ranges since it must be sufficiently capable of being extended to those who will complement it, to the "representative segment" through "market research"; it will build the scenarios you want to reach and the unstoppable way in which you face your reality.

The mettle given by the intention will always be reflected in "your loyal consumer" that contains the mix of action elaborated and directed by your professional structure, with the requested reaction of your representative segment. Accumulation that must now be especially well translated, exceeding both expectations so that they culminate in the correct cooling of the combined equipment.

Your ices are the intention that you grant to each of the elements that you develop in your company, and that is especially reflected in the translation of "design requirements" as the reflection of wanting to win that is addressed to the consumer and is collected from. Your ice must be the most complete, crystalline and cold.

3.   Tequila:

As the first active ingredient in Sunrise you must pour all the structure with which you have to create and translate all your plans. If you do not know why your company does not work as you want and you want to have everything in order, the configuration of the mission, vision and values that support your business must change through your "corporate presence" to project it as a stronger base of support. For this you require a solid "business plan" which is the structure with the objectives of your company, only if you know how your company is structured and how it works from its foundations to its latest repercussions, is that you can have total control over what you have, to build and get to what you want to achieve. There are no limits to achieve your projects, you can change, improve and create the most complete and firm administration you can imagine; just knowing. If you know what and how you are holding in detail, you will understand how easy it is to operate the ideal structure necessary in your company, to set corporate goals and use of the strategy homogeneously inside and outside your company.

In this way you achieve its projection where the analysis of its internal and external environments "SWOT" intervenes, with which in addition to involving your capital and human talent, you invite all participants within the sector to compete, a level in which in the first place you must take into account the public that is the main spectator of each movement that your company shows. This is where the *presence-expectation* exchange arises, where the public expects to receive benefits from what the presence that they see being planted sells.

These processes must develop and maintain great support for your "corporate identity", this is the visual representation of your company that formally projects its planted conduct towards the sector and establishes the mentality with which it addresses towards its target audience. Designing your corporate identity must be based on the analysis of your entire strategic process, where your mission, vision, values and philosophy build the form of visual communication as they will see your company and relate an identity supported by the strength of the "character" that is projects.

Your tequila must be the structural base of your company, it represents the presence face to the sector and your target audience. The best house tonic.

Ingredient that corresponds to the administration. It is which effectively represents the strength that requires your company. And as the support that needs to have broad and unique qualities to forever remain standing, from your place of business you must observe the movements of the sector where you stand with your plan to contend with those who are using the perfect combination, and stand firm. Get your company to achieve strong presence since from your startup and your position will be watched by an audience that is eager to find a structure that can to shelter as he likes, and is made with Tequila which belongs to Sunrise.

The distilled served as the first discipline than kicks in, builds the initial organizational basis of any business, from where it develops:

a)	The strategic management process.

b)	And the use of the SWOT analysis: Balancing environments, internal according to the objectives of the organization and external to propose their strategy in the sector of competitiveness, in an appropriate manner, with the approach of "all depends on."

Each company must submit its strategic management process with the development of its mission, vision, philosophy and objectives, supports the name of your firm, corporate identity, and corporate colors, your website should reflect a general reaffirmation of it, which must be as homogeneous as each other to effectively reach to your target audience; that is their projection. And your portfolio should show their technique and its trajectory that raise its category on the market, is the characteristic way to get better positioning than its competition in the industry; that is his strategy.

4.	Orange:

With this active ingredient of the cocktail you must show with what characteristics you are going to develop the product or service that you want to put on the market most convenient for consumption. All business projects must be based on knowledge of what the consumer demands, fresh information obtained from the target audience who will be the one to obtain, enjoy and judge the qualities of your product. The best insight you can get to gather sentiments and incorporate them into your company's business goals is from the chosen "representative segment" that will give you the first and most faithful first-hand evidence, containing those requested characteristics. For this you must apply a malleable "market study", from this document you will know the requirements that the profile of respondents has created results among which you will especially know important details that your target market prefers about the product and its attributes. You must know precisely the ways and moments in which your prospect feels most familiar with your product and also at which point he is most likely to appropriate it as his own so that at a certain moment he can enjoy it and be satisfied with it. The study must know how the consumer feels what your product will be.

Knowing the market is a revealing point. You must know to project the pertinent actions of the market management of your company by activating the "4 P's" that allow direct interaction with the target market and obtain its response to the stimuli that affect its satisfaction. It will permeate the way in which the implementation of the project, translated into items and audiovisual content of the company, must be approached to the prospect; he objective of "marketing" is fulfilled by preserving the *experience-satisfaction* exchange in brand renewals on market demands. When the target market gets its first successful experience as a result of the genuineness exchanges.

The strategic sense of marketing should move through your brand, which is the visual representation that inherits the character of your company to a certain extent and is linked to feelings towards the target market, constituting its values and its own identity as a brand. It is essential to design the "brand identity" that your product will require, based on it you will establish the sentimental contact that your target market requests with which you will acquire a certain price, you will be able to be the object of a better promotion and you will be able to locate yourself in a place to its distribution, will thus be conducive to communicating the "love" that generates identity and loyalty.

Your orange must be the malleable link of your company, the identity between the objectives and the demands of the target market. The natural juice that concentrates the flavors.

Ingredient that corresponds to marketing. It is which effectively represents the malleability that requires your company. And as the link that needs to have broad and unique qualities to forever adapting to changes consumption, from your place of business you must observe the movements of the market where you stand to know the segment to which you will apply your research and keep that in the sight. Chose well and approach the representative public who is congruent to the purpose you pursue reaching, since you'll be watching for that, the segment from which you will get the best valuable impressions, depends on an accurate projection of the study on contact, to give in mental target from which you can extract the information that consumers want to vent to obtain that which they like demand, and is made with Orange which belongs to Sunrise.

The spill juice, as the second discipline that is activated, strengthens the various connections that will give mobility toward markets, to jump-start:

a)   The marketing management process.

b)   And the marketing mix: Using the 4 P's to analyze the situation and design strategies to achieve profitable organizational objectives and satisfy the real needs of consumers.

Each company must hold its marketing management process in the planning of marketing their services, a high development of balance cost-satisfaction and a detailed direction of the marketing mix towards a satisfactory volume, as a link between company-consumer; that is your advantage. The market planning must be based on the study of its possibilities and the conversion of context to content, driven towards the base for win, that is the consumer, in the consistent way to move the dexterity of marveling at a market in their mobility environment; there it is your competitiveness.

5.   Grenadine:

When pouring this syrup, you must capture consumer preferences and translate them as the "study results." With them you will reflect the characteristics of their emotions; based on its translation and adaptation, you will have on hand all the elements that will endow your product with the visual possibilities that will align with the company's objectives to shape personality and DNA of the product. You will obtain a result that shares company characteristics and confers the desirable nature of the final consumer, the translation of the results of the study must be communicated scrupulously. The key is to apply what you know and improve what you now know, so that it empowers. For this you have to make a correct use of the "brief," this important writing document of the requirements of your product is of invaluable help, with which you will translate from concepts into functional, aesthetic and emotional attributes all the demands that a consumer may wish based on its careful monitoring, you will be able to obtain a well-contextualized product that to a greater extent must be satisfactory and if it is possible to exceed expectations, to reflect them in the increase in sales and in the recommendation of the product when putting it in front of the consumer.

And for this you must activate the design project management process, with which the real parameters of the project are extended in order to circulate the *effect-emotion* exchange in the consumer's mind. When it is already a fact that the effects of the preparation have begun to rise in the mind of the prospect as attractive to his life, that satisfaction is being caused. Thus, based on the company's objectives and the translation of the brief, you must apply the "design strategy" through its strategic process addressing the Level, Environment, Strategy and Implementation "(LESI)" of the project towards its renewal or continuity, based on the promise and perception of the product nurtured with the demands of the consumer; to highlight its values and qualities and endow it with its own personality and adequate communication. Consider analyzing the results.

All this development should result in the "design of your product" which, through acquiring its functional, aesthetic and emotional attributes, will become the focal point that personifies the complete essence of the projected objectives and the requested characteristics helping to determine the purchase. You will have to work to fulfill the central promise of the product, keep in touch with the needs of the prospect and attend to the perception of the product against the emotions of the consumer to turn them into "attitude".

Your grenadine must be the forceful contact of your company, the emotional attributes of the product for the consumer. The syrup that triggers the impact on the mind.

Ingredient that corresponds to design. It is effectively representing the impact that requires your company. And as the trigger that need extensive and unique qualities to always carry what they are looking to be the prospectus, from your place of operations for the brief, you must observe their movements on the Internet to introduce you to who are interacting in their relentless pursuit of valuation and stay present. Connect to their principles and be consistent with the arguments required by, as each of them will observe you and represents all turned into buyer, and they are about to become the endorsement to recommend and disseminate their deepest needs to get the qualities of what you have created, a global communication that keeps its promises and adds them as part of them, and is made with Grenadine which belongs to Sunrise.

The syrup served as the third discipline than starts, precipitates the plans for representing through image communication to the final consumer, and impels:

a)   The design projects management process.

b)   And the proper use of briefing or design requirements: The ability to define entrepreneurs and members of the company all the objectives and requirements of the project.

Every company should be aware of their design projects management process, based on the fulfillment of its objectives, the project development emphasizing the importance of using the briefing, and overall analysis of its results, involving all those people join in the project with respect to consumer demands; that is their differentiation. Design feature is to be functional and aesthetic, capture the essence of desires that generate consumer loyalty and adapt to a context familiar to him and his life, the mode of excite a consumer within its contextual sphere; that is their innovation.

6.   Start the Sunrise Effect:

You must achieve this by giving rise to the concern of owning your product and its promised emotional attributes in the greatest number of prospects, during the different moments of truth from the "Stimulus," the one that emits an item or content when telling a valuable and true story about your "product;" it is from that "instant" created in time which may be before, from launch, or later, that the Sunrise Effect must be kept as a constant emotion and present within the prospect's mind.

If your conformation of Tequila Sunrise for Business is correct, it should undoubtedly cause it to have lasting effects on the prospect and direct at every moment of the truth "initiating the Sunrise Effect;" it will be effective when it remains faithful from the stimulus until it rises to the mind of the prospect, taking place there within the sunrise that verifies its promised attributes.

Your effect should be a catalyst for your company and shocking for the prospect, who approves at all times a: good, very good, better, excellent, ha ha!

7.   Raise the Sunrise Effect:

With the Sunrise Effect barely addressed in the prospect's mind, their immediate response should be achieved by motivating them to consult the product online to find the promise that it has not yet proven, but possibly will fill their need to possess it, spending one by one the moments of the truth until he confirms his awakened qualities from the moment the Stimulus occurs and through an increase in his emotions. From "ZMOT, FMOT, SMOT, to TMOT".

For this, each MOT must preserve and, what better to increase consumer confidence despite the presence of other products, until convincing them that: the acquisition they will make or have made is what they expected and their full satisfaction to guarantee it.

Your MOTs must be able to "elevate the Sunrise Effect" high in the mind of the prospect and subsequent consumer. They should create a joyous coexistence by tasting prospects and consumers with the Sunrise.

8.   Spread the Sunrise Effect:

When finally, the consumer of the product has gone through all the moments of truth satisfactorily and is completely convinced of the product, and its emotional attributes are made reality to satisfy their need, then they must become a guarantee and now go on to recommend the same product.

For this, when the consumer returns to the ZMOT, they must now express their opinion of their experience with the product and advise in the interaction with a new prospect whom wish to consult, and with the power of the consummate Sunrise Effect in the mind of the now endorsement, this can convert another loyal consumer, thus, "spreading the Sunrise Effect."

The Sunrise Effect must have the quality of making a unique impression from the first arrival at the "ZMOT" in its consultation, to be the same on its second visit, now to be shared by who should make it known the maximum party generated by trying the Tequila Sunrise for Business, without knowing that it is contained in a final product.

When a company hits in its sector of mobility (their entity), causes adjustments in their competitiveness environment (their context) and effects on their spheres of perceptibility (their preference); it is because underpins the implementation of the three main disciplines that drive their business, to apply them in their logical sequence from the projection of its dominant process, that is, depending on the process to start a business project the outlook for the other two processes is displayed that consequently take their proper place, adopting the organizational functions that highlights the most important activities that a company requires: to their sector, their environment and context.

Within the development of these disciplines, it is also important establish a determinant behavior to spread as a parameter of the entire company:

1.   In formulating a consistent distribution of management in the operation of its structure.

That is rounded in strategic management, so that it shows great control of his abilities and great presence of their strengths to the thought of context, in order to reach customers world class whether you work for corporate or promoting their own products. Convincing as firm to the largest audience of a particular market segment, intending to spread globally.

2.   When driving a marketing consistent effort in the proposal of their dynamism.

That is supported by strategic marketing so that transfer high conviction pleasurable experiences that give dynamism to the feelings through the stories told, with the intention of achieving a link between the identity of the company, the brand, and the consumer through rapprochement value contents. Tasks to be performed with direct media and specific.

3.   When submitting a differentiator design proposal consistent with their communication.

That is focused on image enhancements of the products and services that display its aesthetic and functional aspects of affective-emotional nature with the purpose of sharing the tangible attributes which give sense of belonging and self-satisfaction and manage to fill their deepest needs of reinvention, dominion, security, and connection through direct contact with consumer demands.

Thus, deep inquiry into each development defines a particular intensity in the business result, leading as a third step, the constant demand for talent applied to maximize the proactive diversity that requires each new project, where you must pay attention to:

1.   The strategic performance of the project:

Highlighting in the company an important development of its corporate goals by which to expand their business activities on the performance areas where they are more focused and supported it, leaving a strong evidence of them in each project specifically in the skills that they were targeted (the implementation of strategies), in building their overall performance (the application of competences) and in the effect of the final results (the implementation of innovations), same elements that reflect its vision and mission, consistently with the important role they play in the market, and the good use of their own design process. The development of briefing is paramount in adapting to changes in obtaining information regardless of the type of project.

2.   The competitive environment analysis:

Each company must show great attention to changes in consumption that could generate the results of the brand or product designed. Their analysis will add the relevant competences and decrease unnecessary under the conditions of briefing, also examines the dose of the ingredients of Sunrise for Business that were implemented to the project. Whether for new launches, when requiring renovation, or adding new elements of communication, these tools play an important role first to identify the best solution to your requirements and then to see how successful was this choice. Each product has certain qualities that must be renewed, the fact overcome them makes compete with renewed mettle increasingly adapted to their context.

3.   The innovations applied to products:

Innovations are an important tool for products and services as a great consumer appeal. Although the needs of each product are varied and also tend to be aimed at different market segments, only those relevant changes in the products are those that help them compete, aspect which shows that however small or large it is a change, there is behind a study that supports its effectiveness and why sometimes projects last months. Applied innovations will allow highlight how satisfied consumer preferences.

Regardless of specialization in any of the areas of design performance, in the different companies must employ the three performances mentioned in the most appropriate manner from the status of renewal of a product, namely, that depending on the improvements required for each brand it is makes sense the implementation of the strategy, innovation, and competitiveness as well as their level of performance in every product.

And thus, as the fourth step is required a high degree of professionalism:

1. Putting in place the strategies:

a) The directives, that command the correct trajectory of design project in the company.

b) Of communication, that intensify product opportunities in the market.

c) The visual, allowing mental association of functional-emotional-aesthetical appealing to the consumer.

2. By providing competitiveness in:

a) The way the business conduct is administered to realize the project, keeping a customer, and impact the consumer to strengthen itself in the market.

b) The ability to manage marketing to get the project, give it capabilities that will position in the market and achieve their effects on the consumer.

c) The perspicacity into the use of design to formulate emotional atmospheres that cause change and to cope with the changes achieved market trends required by the consumer.

3. Accompanying opportunely with innovations:

a) In the administration, since allow better methods emerge for efficiency and effectiveness of the business.

b) In marketing, when formulating the most attractive conditions for global communication about the project.

c) In design, based on new connotations that are not present and will be unique characteristics of the product.

ARTIUX

Basic Concept: The process of managing business projects requires the joint work of the administration, marketing and design. As strategic forces, competitive advantages and differentials innovations, at the corporate level, management, functional and operational.

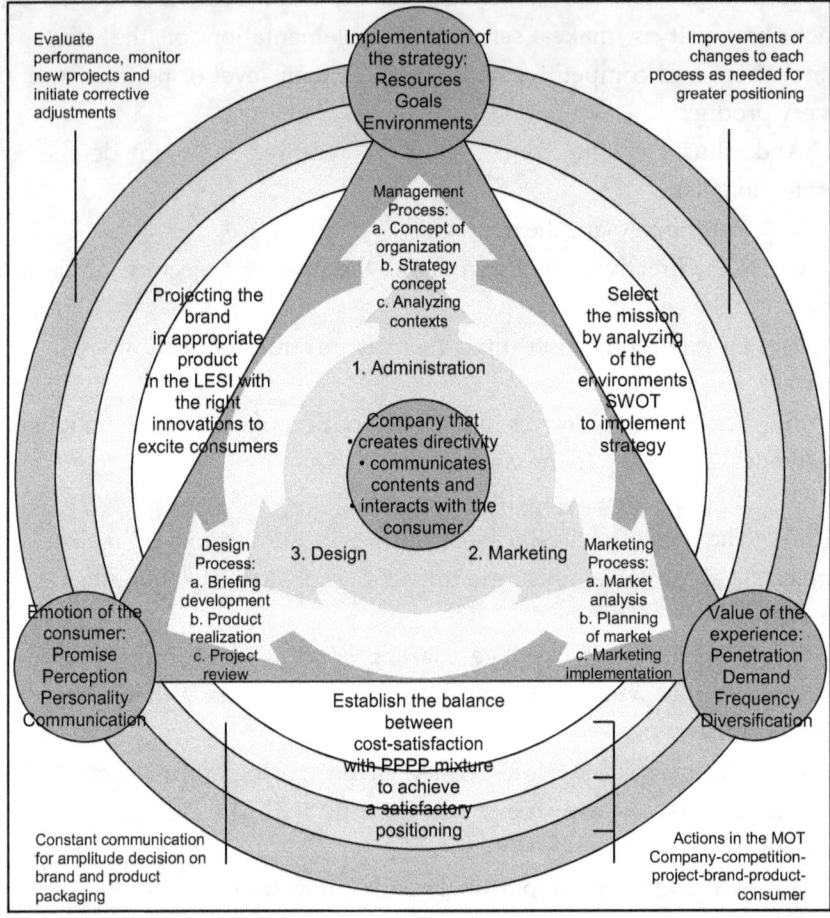

The Matrix of the three management processes in a company. They are cyclical functions of business management to achieve the proposed objectives.

A bite of decorated
The orange and cherry

The question is not: will you succeed? But rather,
will you matter?
SETH GODIN
American author, entrepreneur, marketer, and public speaker

The decoration has a great role to be to your liking at first sight, to accompany a pleasant tasting of the cocktail, and delight your palate when you taste at the end; these three forms are used to generally identify the cocktail and remain impressed in your mind as a unique experience. That experience you rejoice, becomes unforgettable in your mind when after enjoying their tastes run to the final bite that closes with a flourish your personalized reality, in summary, tells you all you remember the content since you saw her initial presentation, when you ingested completely, and until you felt its effect to make it part of you appropriating it you with a bite given to life.

So, I want you to have this summary present to start your own combination.

Remember, to fully develop the Tequila Sunrise for Business must concentrate all the elements required and serve the ingredients in the right order, that way you'll have on hand the arguments to control the preparation and effect. So far, your party is just beginning.

To continue, you will know the description of the bite that you require to keep aware, is a review of the Tequila Sunrise for Business, the idea of this is assimilate the main components to keep into mind and make run all needs the cocktail, I strongly suggest you pay attention to this extract to assimilate all development effectively and make your business a more paradisiacal and lasting scenery for enjoying.

And to have effect on your company develop it properly:

KEYS:	CONTAINS:	TRANSLATE TO:
Tumbler:	Your professional structure	Business plan
Ice cubes:	Your representative segment	Market research
Ice cubes:	Your faithful consumer	Briefing
INGREDIENT:	ACTIVE FORM:	REPRESENTATIVE PATTERN:
Tequila:	Management (SWOT)	Corporate identity & Enterprise
Orange:	Marketing (4 P's)	Brand & Contents video
Grenadine:	Design (LESI)	Brand identity & Product
TRIGGER in:	REFLECTED in:	SATISFY when:
Starting SE:	Stimulus: Moment + Product	Sunrise is introduced to mind
Raising SE:	ZMOT, FMOT, SMOT, TMOT	Customer become endorsement
Spreading SE:	Return to ZMOT to share	Convert more consumers
IT OBTAINED AS A RESULT		
Development of the Tequila Sunrise for Business		

This combined energy is an empowered state of your mind that is focused on your business project, and carried out in big, is therefore, converted into an empowered state of the collective mind concentrated in the commercial system and with which you go to move your business.

And, through the domain of the character, love, and attitude your company gets one thing: success.

When you provoke the consumer to fall in love with it, follow and do follow the evidence of the Tequila Sunrise for Business.

Note that properly prepare the Tequila Sunrise for Business will contain the specific characteristics of each company, reflected in the congruent construction of the product design and Stimulus, so that these two elements contain the qualities of the Tequila Sunrise, and are projecting the emotional benefits to obtain the Sunrise Effect at crucial Moments Of Truth, wherein the Sunrise Effect will rise one by one on the consumer's mind until the effect of the purchased product is up in the minds of consumers when the emotional benefits promised by the product are checked and are finally endorsed by him, causing recommend the product, sharing to a new prospect already tested the

Sunrise Effect, who certainly also will check, will rise to his mind and become a loyal consumer more.

The constant imperative has always been to obtain consumer information, only now stands first, the moment of which should be taken, is from ZMOT, and then is the challenge of how to do it well, attending the emotional benefits that rise to the mind of consumer to incorporate to take effect in new products that promote and impact on consumer habits.

In summary, (quoted in Taylor & Shaw, 1990) "there are three types of companies, those that make things happen, those who watch things happen and those who wonder what happened." (Anonymous)

It has been a pleasure for me having prepared this cocktail, you've come to the bar, and have enjoyed it as a prelude to the party that proposes the commercial system, mastering in business. Now is the time to prepare it well chilled and put it to take effect, to bring up the sun in the mind your next similar, that instead of turning him only into your consumer, be a collaborator more of your business to expand them for the purpose that you win and make him win in the day by day to get what you want to achieve.

This is the preparation of a delicious combination of three ancestral ingredients converted into classics, to be efficient and win in business as is required on a large scale and attract consumers of the international market, which everybody should taste.

Cocktail that depends on you to dominate it, and if you allow it from now on, you can to prepare with mastery and at deeper levels. So that it helps you to discover how you can achieve what you ultimately look for in you too, get the Sunrise.

Bibliography

1.   AMA.org. (2004, October). *About AMA*. Retrieved July 30, 2013, from Definition of Marketing: https://www.ama.org/AboutAMA/Pages/Definition-of-Marketing.aspx

2.   AMA.org. (2014). *Dictionary AMA*. Retrieved October 31, 2014, from Marketing mix: https://www.ama.org/resources/pages/dictionary.aspx?dLetter=M

3.   Aramburuzavala, M. A. (2016, november 22). *Forbes México*. Retrieved from www.youtube.com: https://www.youtube.com/watch?v=fpa3BUdLjJU

4.   Argote, L., & Ingram, P. (2000, May). Knowledge transfer: A basis for competitive advantage in firms. *82*(1), 150-169.

5.   Artiux. (2016). *Design Management in Design Companies of Mexico City*. USA.

6.   Baena, V. (2011). *Fundamentos de marketing: entorno, consumidor, estrategia e investigación comercial [Fundamentals of Marketing: environment, consumer and trade research strategy]*. Barcelona, Spain: Editorial UOC.

7.   Berry, T. (2014, October 13). *Soyentrepreneur.com*. (T. Berry, Editor) Retrieved October 13, 2014, from 8 pasos para escribir tu plan de negocios [8 steps to write your business plan]: http://www.soyentrepreneur.com/27518-8-pasos-para-escribir-tu-plan-de-negocios.html

8.   Bonsiepe, G. (1999). *Del objeto a la interfase: Mutaciones del diseño [Of the object to the interface: Design Mutations]*. Buenos Aires, Argentina: Ediciones Infinito.

9.   Brant, J., & Lohse, S. (2014). *The open innovation model*. Paris, France: International Chamber of Commerce.

10.   Bruce, M., & Bessant, J. (2002). *Design in business. Strategic Innovation Through Design*. London, England: Financial Times-Prentice Hall.

11.   Bruce, M., Cooper, R., & Vazquez, D. (1999). *Effective design management for small businesses* (Vol. 20). Manchester, United Kingdom:

Design Studies.

12. Business Wire. (2017, March 09). *Global Tequila Market Witness Growth 2021*. Retrieved from businesswire.com: https://www.businesswire.com/news/home/20170309005955/en/Global-Tequila-Market-Witness-Growth-2021-Owing

13. Castillo, C., & Bond, F. O. (1987). *The university of Chicago spanish-english english-spanish dictionary*. USA: Pocket Books.

14. Chaves, N. (2001). *El oficio de diseñar. Propuesta a la conciencia crítica de los que comienzan [The profession of designing. Proposal to critical awareness of those who begin]*. Barcelona, Spain: GG Diseño.

15. Chiavenato, I. (2001). *Introducción a la teoría general de la administración [Introduction to general management theory]*. Mexico City, Mexico: McGraw-Hill.

16. Coca Carasila, A. M. (2008, May-August). El concepto de Marketing: pasado y presente [Marketing Concept: Past and Present]. (J. Fuenmayor, Ed.) *Revista de Ciencias Sociales [Journal of Social Sciences]*, 393-395.

17. Cohen, H. (2013, June 27). *Marketing: The 4 Moments of Truth [Chart]*. (L. Aronson, Editor, WebFaction, Producer, & Aweber) Retrieved December 01, 2014, from Marketing's 4 moments of truth defined: http://heidicohen.com/marketing-the-4-moments-of-truth-chart/#sthash.qaOHhTYb.dpuf

18. Colmenares Grünberger, O. (1992). *Administración Estratégica: Casos de Empresas Mexicanas [Strategic Management: Case Mexican Companies]*. Mexico City, Mexico: Edamex.

19. Condusef. (2013). *Empresario PyME como usuarios de servicios financieros [Businessman SMEs as the users of financial services]*. Retrieved October 10, 2014, from Plan de negocios y cómo hacerlo [Business Plan and how to do]: http://www.condusef.gob.mx/index.php/empresario-pyme-como-usuarios-de-servicios-financieros/119-plan-de-negocios-y-como-hacerlo

20. Consejo Regulador del Tequila [Tequila Regulatory Council]. (2013, November 1st). *http://www.crt.org.mx*. Retrieved from Información Estadística [Statistical information]: http://www.crt.org.mx/EstadisticasCRTweb/

21. Contreras, J. (2001). *Administración estratégica [Strategic*

Management]. Mexico City, Mexico: Universidad Nacional Autónoma de México.

22.   Daniels, W. R. (2000, Spring). Meetings build strategic relationships. *Design Management Journal, 11*(2), 63-71.

23.   De Jong, J., Vanhaverbeke, W., Kalvet, T., & Chesbrough, H. (2008). *Policies for open innovation: Theory, framework and cases.* Helsinki, Finland: Research project funded by Vision Era-Net.

24.   Dell, M. (2019, may 26). *www.youtube.com*. Retrieved from The university of Texas at Austin: https://www.youtube.com/watch?v=sIyGA1MlbwY

25.   Donis Dondis, A. (1992). *La sintaxis de la imagen. Introducción al alfabeto visual [A Primer of Visual Literacy].* Mexico City, Mexico: GG Diseño.

26.   Droste, M. (1991). *Bauhaus 1919-1933.* Berlin, Germany: Editorial Archive and Museum of Design Bauhaus.

27.   EducaMarketing. (2005). *Guía para realizar una Investigación de Mercados [Guide to perform a Market Research].* (U. Extremadura, Ed.) Retrieved November 01, 2014, from Área de Comercialización e Investigación de Mercados [Department of Marketing and Market Research]: http://educamarketing.unex.es/Docs/guias/Gu%C3%ADa%20realizaci%C3%B

28.   Ellison, L. (2013, February 23th). Exclusive interview of Larry Ellison - ceo of oracle corp. India: Youtube. Retrieved from https://www.youtube.com/watch?v=OLahcEI--2E&ebc=ANyPxKonJFxix38yRNgpp6BD6D_sjeZbc3bgETS8Xsme3Ugj9j5qbCAtg5BcpOm4f_NUaLlil8A4sOqOrtGvusu_08ZNMDsXzg

29.   Enríquez Morán, C. (2013, October 29). *Forbes.com.mx*. Retrieved from 4 secretos básicos del marketing para PyMEs [4 basic secrets of marketing for SMEs]: http://www.forbes.com.mx/4-secretos-basicos-del-marketing-para-pymes/

30.   Etimonline.com. (2014). *Online Etymology Diccionary*. (D. C. Buglione, Editor, D. McCormack, Producer, & Sponsored Words) Retrieved October 26, 2014, from Market: http://www.etymonline.com/index.php?allowed_in_frame=0&search=market&searchmode=none

31.   Filson, A., & Lewis, A. (2000). Barriers between design and business strategy. *Design Management Journal, 11*(4), 48-52.

32.   Fischer De la Vega, L., & Espejo Callado, J. (2004). *Mercadotecnia [Marketing]* (3rd ed.). Mexico City, Mexico: Mc Graw Hill.

33.   Fisher De la Vega, L. (1988). *Mercadotecnia [Marketing].* Mexico City, Mexico: Interamericana.

34.   Free-management-ebooks.com. (2013). *Ansoff Matrix. Strategy Skills.* Warwickshire, United Kingdom: free-management-ebooks.com.

35.   Frías, J. (2004, February 14). Administración del diseño [Design management]. (A. Pérez Iragorri, Ed.) *a! Diseño*(67), 57-59. Retrieved Noviembre 10, 2007, from http://www.a.com.mx

36.   Fuentes, V. (2013, January 10). Las marcas más poderosas [The most powerful brands]. (J. F. López, Ed.) *Poder y Negocios [Power and Business magazine],* 1, 28-32, 34 http://www.mediasolutions.com.mx/ncpop.asp?n=201310090057014801 &t=.

37.   García Padilla, V. M. (2014). *Introducción a las finanzas [Introduction to Finance].* Mexico City, Mexico: Grupo Editorial Patria.

38.   Gombrich, E. H. (1999). *La historia del arte [The history of art].* Mexico City, Mexico: Conaculta-Editorial Diana.

39.   González, C. (2004, February 14). Design Bureau. Entrevista a Carlos González Nacif [Design Bureau. Interview with Carlos González Nacif]. (A. Pérez Iragorri, Ed.) *a! Diseño*(67), 41-47. Retrieved september 16, 2008, from http://www.a.com.mx

40.   Grefé, R. (1997). *Design culture. An anthology of writing from the AIGA journal of graphic design.* (S. Heller, Ed.) New York, USA: Allwort Press.

41.   Guijosa, V., & Frías, J. (2006, January 15). Administración del diseño [Design management]. (A. Pérez Iragorri, Ed.) *a! Diseño*(77), 77-79. Retrieved August 23, 2007, from http://www.a.com.mx

42.   Hauser, A. (1978). *Historia social de la literatura y del arte [Social history of literature and art]* (Vol. 1). Madrid, Spain: Guadarrama Punto Omega.

43.   Hill, C. W., & Jones, G. R. (2005). *Administración estratégica. Un enfoque integrado [Strategic Management: An Integrated Approach].* Mexico City, Mexico: McGraw Hill Interamericana.

44. Idologie.com. (2012). *Proceso [Process]*. (X. Olguín, Producer) Retrieved October 15, 2014, from mapa/breif [map/briefing]: http://www.idologie.com/proceso.html

45. Iduarte, J., & Zarza, M. (2004). *La administración del diseño en micro pequeñas y medianas empresas mexicanas [The design management in micro small and medium Mexican companies]*. Autonomous University of Estado de México, Faculty of Architecture and Design. Toluca: UAEM. Retrieved 07 10, 2006, from http://www.dis.uia.mx/conference/2005/HTMs-PDFs/AdmondelDisenoenEmpresas.pdf

46. Isern, A. (2003). *Guía creativity 2003: el diseño y la comunicación en la gestión empresarial [Creativity Guide 2003: design and communication in business management]*. Barcelona, Spain: Guía Creativity.

47. J., Boyd, H., O., W., & Larreché, J. (2007). *Administración de marketing. Un enfoque en la toma estratégica de decisiones. [Marketing Management: A Strategic Decision-Making Approach]*. Mexico City, Mexico: Mc Graw Hil Interamericana.

48. Jeffrey, K. R., & Hunt, D. (1985, Janauary). Design in small manufacturing companies in Scotland. *6*(1), 18-24.

49. Kaplan, A. M. (2014, August). European management and European business schools: Insights from the History of Business Schools. (M. Haenlein, Ed.) *European Management Journal, 32*(4), 529-534.

50. Kirwin, R. (2004, February 14). Marca la diferencia [Mark the difference]. (A. Pérez Iragorri, Ed.) *a! Diseño*(67), 49. Retrieved April 23, 2007, from http://www.a.com.mx

51. Kotler, P. (2009). *Dirección de mercadotecnia [Marketing Management]*. Mexico City, Mexico: Prentice Hall.

52. Kotler, P., & Amstrong, G. (2003). *Fundamentos de marketing [Fundamentals of Marketing]*. Mexico City, Mexico: Pearson Education.

53. Kunst, M. (1995, March-April). Notas para una filosofía del diseño [Notes for a design philosophy]. (L. Moreno, Ed.) *De Diseño, 1*(3), 8-9.

54. La Nación. (2008, June 01). *Joan Costa: El diseño socializa el conocimiento [Joan Costa: Design socializes knowledge]*. Retrieved November 07, 2014, from Enfoques [Approaches]: http://www.lanacion.com.ar/1017188-joan-costa-el-diseno-socializa-el-

conocimiento

55. Lamb, C., Hair, J., & McDaniel, C. (2011). *Marketing*. Mexico City, Mexico: Cengage Learning.

56. Lawrence, P. (1996). Inc. Magazine's George Gendron on design. *@issue. The Journal of Business and Design, 2*(1), 2-5.

57. Lecinski, J. (2011). *ZMOT Ebook: Winning the Zero Moment of Truth.* Illinois, Chicago, USA: Google Inc.

58. Levy, A. R. (1981). *Planeamiento estratégico [Strategic Planning].* Buenos Aires, Argentina: Ediciones Macchi.

59. Licko, Z. (2002, Spring). 'It's not a problem of being a woman in a man's world. It's being a type designer in a world that gives little recognition to this art form'. (J. L. Walters, Ed.) *Eye magazine, 11*(43), http://eyemagazine.com/feature/article/reputations-zuzana-licko.

60. Lupton, E., & Abott, M. J. (1994). *El abc de la Bauhaus y la teoría del diseño [ABC's of the Bauhaus: Bauhaus and Design Theory].* Barcelona, Spain: GG Diseño.

61. Mintzberg, H., Brian, J., & Voyer, J. (1997). *El proceso estratégico. Conceptos, contextos y casos [The Strategy Process: Concepts, Context, Cases].* Mexico City, Mexico: Prentice Hall Hispanoamericana.

62. Mono, D., Rivers, C., & Dowdy, C. (2006). *Identidad corporativa: del brief a la solución final. [Branding: From Brief to Finished Solution].* Barcelona, Spain: GG Diseño.

63. Mullins, J., Boyd, H., O., W., & Larreché, J. (2007). *Administración de marketing. Un enfoque en la toma estratégica de decisiones [Marketing Management: A Strategic Decision-Making Approach].* Mexico City, Mexico: Mc Graw Hil Interamericana.

64. Munch Galindo, L. (2009). *Fundamentos de administración [Management foundations].* Mexico City, Mexico: Trillas.

65. Muñoz, P. (2007, September 20). X_Design. Estrategias para llegar a grandes clientes [Strategies to reach large customers]. (A. Pérez Iragorri, Ed.) *a! Diseño*(86), 30-37. Retrieved December 04, 2007, from http://www.a.com.mx

66. Musk, E. (2014, May 16th). Elon Musk USC Commencement Speech | USC Marshall School of Business Undergraduate Commencement 2014. Los Angeles, California, USA: Youtube. Retrieved from https://www.youtube.com/watch?v=e7Qh-vwpYH8

67. Myownbusiness.org. (2013, December 12). *Session 2: The Business Plan*. Retrieved October 13, 2014, from What is a business plan?: http://www.myownbusiness.org/espanol/s2/#1

68. Nafinsa. (2009). *www.nafin.gob.mx*. (NacionalFinanciera, Ed.) Retrieved from 13 Pasos para Hacer tu Plan de Negocios [13 Steps to Make Your Business Plan]: www.nafin.gob.mx/portalnf/get?file=/pdf/otros/TRECE-PASOS.pdf

69. O'Reilly, J. (2002). *Sin briefing: proyectos personales de diseñadores gráficos [No Brief: Graphic Designers' Personal Projects]*. Spain: Index Book.

70. Olson, E., Slater, S., & Cooper, R. (2000). Managing design for competitive advantage. *Design Managament Journal, 11*(4), 10-17.

71. Organization for Economic Co-operation and Development. (2005). *Oslo Manual: Guidelines for Collecting and Interpreting Innovation Data*. European Commission: OECD Publishing.

72. Pérez Iragorri, A. (Ed.). (2007, March 20). La psicología del color en el producto [The psychology of color in the product]. *a! Diseño*(83), 59. Retrieved July 13, 2007, from http://www.a.com.mx

73. Phoenixnewtimes. (2015). *http://www.phoenixnewtimes.com*. Retrieved from arts/the-biltmore-original-tequila-sunrise: http://www.phoenixnewtimes.com/arts/the-biltmore-original-tequila-sunrise-6570176

74. Porter, M. E. (1980). *Competitive strategy: Techniques for Analyzing Industries and Competitiors*. New York, USA: The Free Press.

75. Porter, M. E. (1990). *La ventaja competitiva de las naciones [The competitive advantage of nations]*. Buenos Aires, Argentina: Vergara Editor.

76. Porter, M., & Scott, S. (2001, Summer). Innovation: Location Matters. *MIT Sloan Management Review, 42*(4), 28.

77. RAE. (2012). *Diccionario de la Real Academia Española [Dictionary of the Royal Spanish Academy]*, 22nd Edition. Retrieved November 5, 2014, from Mercadotecnia [Marketing]: http://lema.rae.es/drae/?val=mercadotecnia

78. RAE. (2012). *Diccionario de la Real Academia Española [Dictionary of the Royal Spanish Academy]*, 22nd Edition. Retrieved October 31, 2014, from Innovación [Innovation]: http://lema.rae.es/drae/?val=innovación

79. revistafortuna. (2013, February 20th). *http://revistafortuna.com.mx*.

Retrieved from el tequila siempre nuestro [tequila always our]:
http://revistafortuna.com.mx/contenido/2013/02/20/el-tequila-
siempre-nuestro/

80.   Rodríguez Morales, L. (1989). *Para una teoría del diseño [For a design theory]*. Mexico City, Mexico: Tilde-UAM Azcapotzalco.

81.   Saínz de Vicuña Ancín, J. M. (2013). *El plan de marketing en la práctica [The marketing plan in practice]*. Madrid, Spain: ESIC.

82.   Santesmases, M., Sánchez, A., & Valderrey, F. (2003). *Mercadotecnia. Conceptos y estrategias [Marketing. Concepts and strategies]*. Mexico City: ITESM – Pirámide.

83.   Satué, E. (1988). *El diseño gráfico: desde los orígenes hasta nuestros días [Graphic design: from the origins to the present day]*. Madrid, Spain: Alianza.

84.   Schmidt, E. E. (2012, may 20). *Boston University*. Retrieved from www.youtube.com: https://www.youtube.com/watch?v=GZRIMQxje7k

85.   Schoell, W. F., & Guiltinan, J. P. (1991). *Mercadotecnia. Conceptos y prácticas modernas [Marketing. Modern concepts and practices]*. Mexico City: Prentice Hall Hispanoamericana.

86.   Schultz, H. (2017, may 09). *Starbucks Coffee*. Retrieved from www.youtube.com: https://www.youtube.com/watch?v=NVekVtJ4104

87.   Schumpeter, J. A. (1978). *Teoría del desenvolvimiento económico [Theory of economic development]* (Fifth reprint ed.). Mexico City, Mexico: Fondo de Cultura Económica.

88.   Slim, C. (2017, october 31). *carloslimvideoficial*. Retrieved from www.youtube.com: https://www.youtube.com/watch?v=ENEXHW0x8dQ

89.   Smith, F. (2013, april 17). *Tajeviblog*. Retrieved from www.youtube.com: https://www.youtube.com/watch?v=TvspHKQ6WZo

90.   Sobrino, R., & Mercado, F. (2006, January 15). Marketing Design. (A. Pérez Iragorri, Ed.) *a! Diseño*(77), 74-76. Retrieved March 20, 2007, from http://www.a.com.mx

91.   Stanton, W., Etzel, M., & Walker, B. (2007). *Fundamentos de Marketing [Fundamentals of Marketing]* (13th ed.). Mexico City, Mexico: Mc Graw Hill-Interamericana.

92.   Taylor, J. W., & Shaw, T. R. (1990). *Mercadotecnia: un enfoque integrador [Marketing: an integrative approach].* Mexico City, Mexico: Trillas.

93.   Telford, A. (2001, March-April). Diseño en México [Design in Mexico]. (C. &. Blanchard, Ed.) *Communication Arts, 43*(1), 115-130.

94.   Thompson, A., & Strickland, A. J. (1998). *Dirección y administración estratégicas: conceptos, casos y lecturas [Strategic Manaement: concepts, cases and readings]* (first edition ed.). Mexico City, Mexico: McGraw Hill.

95.   Thompson, A., & Strickland, A. J. (2004). *Strategic management. Concepts and cases.* USA: Mc Graw Hill.

96.   UL. (1973, March). Acquainted elements to fall down a swing. *University of London Newsletter*, 53.

97.   Wang, C. (2018, february 27). *HTC VIVE.* Retrieved from www.youtube.com: https://www.youtube.com/watch?v=mpxZmBw4FWc

98.   Wikipedia.org. (2015, January 13). *Competitividad [Competitiviness].* Retrieved January 13, 2015 at 07:13, from Wikipedia, The Free Encyclopedia: http://es.wikipedia.org/wiki/Competitividad

99.   Wikipedia.org. (2015, February 13). *Diseño gráfico [Graphic Design].* Retrieved February 13, 2015 at 15:07, from Wikipedia, The Free Encyclopedia: http://es.wikipedia.org/wiki/Diseño_gráfico

100. Wikipedia.org. (2015, January 20). *Negocio [Business].* Retrieved January 24, 2015 at 14:27, from Wikipedia, The Free Encyclopedia: http://es.wikipedia.org/wiki/Negocio

101. Wikipedia.org. (2015, May 21). *Tequila Sunrise (cocktail).* Retrieved from Wikipedia, The Free Encyclopedia: https://en.wikipedia.org/wiki/Tequila_Sunrise_(cocktail)

102. Wingler, H. M. (1975). *Bauhaus. Weimar Dessau Berlin 1919-1933.* Barcelona, Spain: GG Diseño.

103. Wong, W. (1995). *Fundamentos del diseño [Principles of form and design].* Mexico City, Mexico: GG Diseño.

104. Zimmermann, Y. (1998). *Del diseño [Of the design].* Barcelona, Spain: GG Diseño.

105. Zuckerberg, M. (2017, may 25). *Harvard University.* Retrieved from www.youtube.com:

https://www.youtube.com/watch?v=BmYv8XGl-YU

About the author

From 1999 to 2010 I was a teacher in some educational institutions in Mexico City. I have over 20 years of integrated design experience and a Bachelor of Graphic Design from *Universidad Nacional Autónoma de México* (*UNAM*) [National Autonomous University of Mexico]. Today I work as an independent for my own projects from my place of residence. I show clients and followers cope with the challenges in all phases of personal development to business to achieve success.